Betty Crocker

Learn with Betty

ESSENTIAL RECIPES AND TECHNIQUES TO BECOME A CONFIDENT COOK

Houghton Mifflin Harcourt
Boston   New York   2018

GENERAL MILLS

Global Business Solutions Director:
Heather Polen

Global Business Solutions Manager:
Maja Qamar

Executive Editor:
Cathy Swanson Wheaton

Recipe Development and Testing:
Betty Crocker Kitchens

Photography: General Mills Photography
Studios and Image Library

HOUGHTON MIFFLIN HARCOURT

Editorial Director: Deb Brody

Executive Editor: Anne Ficklen

Editorial Associate: Sarah Kwak

Managing Editor: Marina Padakis

Production Editor: Helen Seachrist

Art Director: Tai Blanche

Cover Design: Allison Chi

Interior Design and Layout: Allison Chi

Senior Production Coordinator:
Kimberly Kiefer

For information about permission to reproduce selections
from this book, write to trade.permissions@hmhco.com or to
Permissions, Houghton Mifflin Harcourt Publishing Company,
3 Park Avenue, New York, New York 10016.

hmhco.com

Library of Congress Cataloging-in-Publication Data

Names: Crocker, Betty, author. | Betty Crocker Kitchens.

Title: Betty Crocker learn with Betty : essential recipes and
the techniques to become a confident cook.

Description: Boston : Houghton Mifflin Harcourt, 2018. |
Includes index.

Identifiers: LCCN 2017059044 (print) | LCCN 2017058455
(ebook) | ISBN 9781328503831 (ebook) | ISBN 9781328497673
(paper over board)

Subjects: LCSH: Cooking. | LCGFT: Cookbooks.

Classification: LCC TX714 (print) | LCC TX714 .C7517 2018
(ebook) | DDC 641.5—dc23

LC record available at https://lccn.loc.gov/2017059044

Manufactured in China

C&C 10 9 8 7 6 5 4 3 2 1

Interior and endpaper illustrations: primiaou / Shutterstock
.com

The Betty Crocker Kitchens seal
guarantees success in your kitchen.
Every recipe has been tested in
America's Most Trusted Kitchens™ to
meet our high standards of reliability,
easy preparation and great taste.

FIND MORE GREAT IDEAS AT
BettyCrocker.com

Dear Friends,

Preparing enticing food that you can share with family and friends is pure joy! Your satisfaction is complete when you serve recipes that taste amazing and you get murmurs of "*mmm,*" "this is great"—or better yet, empty plates or requests to share your recipes!

It's a simple equation: irresistible dishes = wonderful conversation + laughter + memories in the making.

Whether you are brand-new to cooking or you've been around the kitchen a few times, you'll love this hand-selected essential recipe collection that will be your go-to resource no matter what the occasion. Learn to master these can't-go-wrong recipes with our terrific tips, tricks and helpful how-tos; then get chefy! Each recipe also includes five ways to change it up with new ingredients to make it different every time. That's *an additional 310 recipes* to add variety and let your creativity loose.

This book doesn't stop there. We've also included inspiring-but-doable features to help you even more. Feel confident whipping up your own creations with our **Customizable Muffins** (page 192), **Build a Delicious Salad** (page 164) or **Throw Together an Amazing Charcuterie Board** (page 44). Use our **Party-Ready in 30 Minutes** guide (page 236) for hosting an impromptu gathering—right from your pantry! Or host Thanksgiving with success with our **How to Pull Off Thanksgiving Dinner cheat sheet** (page 118). It breaks down hosting Thanksgiving into an easy-to-follow checklist so your guests will be impressed and you'll score big for the effort.

Let us help you be a success in the kitchen and an awesome host or hostess! Everything you need to pull off fantastic meals and gatherings is right here, ready for you.

Let's get cooking!

Betty Crocker

Contents

KILLER
Appetizers

GUACAMOLE

2 CUPS DIP   PREP TIME: **15 MINUTES**   START TO FINISH: **15 MINUTES**

1 **small jalapeño chile***

2 **ripe large avocados**

2 **tablespoons fresh lime or lemon juice**

2 **tablespoons finely chopped red onion**

2 **tablespoons finely chopped fresh cilantro**

¼ to ½ **teaspoon salt**

Dash pepper

1 **small clove garlic, finely chopped**

1 **small tomato, seeded, chopped (½ cup)**

Tortilla chips, if desired

1. Remove stems, seeds and ribs from chile; chop chile. Cut avocados lengthwise in half; remove pit and peel. In medium glass or plastic bowl, mash avocados with fork. Immediately toss with lime juice. Gently stir in chile and remaining ingredients except tortilla chips until mixed.

2. Serve with tortilla chips.

*1 tablespoon canned chopped green chiles can be substituted for the jalapeño chile.

1 TABLESPOON: CALORIES 15; TOTAL FAT 1G (SATURATED FAT 0G, TRANS FAT 0G); CHOLESTEROL 0MG; SODIUM 15MG; TOTAL CARBOHYDRATE 0G (DIETARY FIBER 0G); PROTEIN 0G **EXCHANGES:** FREE **CARBOHYDRATE CHOICES:** 0

Techniques

WORKING WITH AVOCADOS

- Look for avocados without bruises, soft spots or loose skin. Avoid if the stem end shows decay. Ripe avocados yield to gentle pressure.
- To ripen, let stand at room temperature in a closed paper bag with a whole kiwifruit or apple (to speed up the ripening process) until ripe. Depending on how hard the avocados are, this may take several days.
- Immediately toss cut avocado with fresh lime or lemon juice to help prevent browning. Press and smooth plastic wrap directly onto surface of leftover guacamole to help prevent discoloration.

CUTTING AVOCADOS

Cut avocado lengthwise through skin around pit.

With hands, slowly twist both sides to separate.

Slide flatware tablespoon under pit to remove.

Make cuts through flesh; scoop out flesh with spoon.

VARIATIONS ▶

Variations

BACON-GUACAMOLE GRILLED CHEESE
When preparing grilled cheese sandwiches, spread the inside of each slice of bread with 1 tablespoon guacamole before topping with cheese. Top cheese with 1 or 2 slices crisply cooked bacon.

FRUITY GUACAMOLE
Gently stir ½ cup finely chopped fruit into guacamole before serving with tortilla chips. Try pineapple (fresh or canned) or fresh mango or strawberries.

GUACAMOLE DEVILED EGGS
Mash the yolks from hard-cooked eggs with fork. Stir in desired amount of the prepared guacamole. Scoop mixture into whites with small spring-handled scoop or spoon. Sprinkle lightly with ground cumin and garnish with chopped cilantro.

MEXICAN GUACAMOLE PASTA
Stir 1 tablespoon olive oil into ¼ cup prepared guacamole until well blended. Toss with 4 cups hot cooked pasta. Toss with ½ cup rinsed and drained canned black beans, 1½ cup chopped tomato, ¼ cup crumbled Cotija or feta cheese and ¼ cup drained canned whole kernel corn.

SHRIMP-GUACAMOLE DIP
Stir ½ (8-ounce) package softened cream cheese until smooth. Fold in ½ cup prepared guacamole. Stir in ⅓ cup peeled deveined finely chopped cooked shrimp. Serve with crackers.

Fresh
TOMATO SALSA

3½ CUPS DIP   PREP TIME: **20 MINUTES**   START TO FINISH: **20 MINUTES**

- **3** large tomatoes, seeded, chopped (3 cups)
- **1** small green bell pepper, chopped (½ cup)
- **8** medium green onions, sliced (½ cup)
- **3** cloves garlic, finely chopped
- **2** tablespoons chopped fresh cilantro
- **1** tablespoon finely chopped jalapeño chile
- **2 to 3** tablespoons fresh lime juice
- **½** teaspoon salt

1. In medium glass or plastic bowl, mix all ingredients.

2. Cover and let stand at room temperature up to 2 hours, or refrigerate until serving. Best used within 1 to 2 days.

¼ CUP: CALORIES 15; TOTAL FAT 0G (SATURATED FAT 0G, TRANS FAT 0G); CHOLESTEROL 0MG; SODIUM 90MG; TOTAL CARBOHYDRATE 2G (DIETARY FIBER 0G); PROTEIN 0G **EXCHANGES:** FREE **CARBOHYDRATE CHOICES:** 0

TEST KITCHEN TIP

Use any tomatoes you have on hand that are in season or on sale at your supermarket. As long as you have 3 cups of chopped tomatoes, it doesn't matter what kind! Try mixing different colored tomatoes for visual variety.

CHOOSING AND STORING TOMATOES

The key to this dish is to choose tomatoes that are flavorful. The better the tomato, the better the salsa!

- Choose firm, unblemished fruit heavy for their size. Tomatoes should smell like tomatoes. If they don't have a scent, they won't have much flavor.
- Store tomatoes at room temperature (refrigerating tomatoes will result in flavor loss). Use within a few days.

CUTTING TOMATOES

- Cut tomatoes with a serrated knife to prevent them from squishing while you cut.
- Cut a thin slice from stem end; set aside.
- Turn tomato cut side down for easier cutting. Cut slices horizontally the thickness you'd like your pieces to be.
- Restack slices if necessary; cut slices into strips the width you'd like your pieces to be by cutting down through slices.
- Stack a few strips at a time; cut crosswise into pieces. Repeat with remaining strips.
- Cut out stem from reserved top slice; discard. Cut remaining top slice into pieces.

CUTTING JALAPEÑOS

To cut jalapeño chiles, wear gloves to keep the invisible oils from burning your fingers and also inadvertently transferring the oils to other parts of your body that you touch.

- Cut chile lengthwise in half; remove the stem and seeds.
- Cut chile lengthwise into strips.
- Cut strips crosswise into pieces.

CHOPPING CILANTRO

When chopping cilantro, you want mostly leaves, but you can chop a few stems as well. You can save the stems for another use, such as making Pesto, page 37.

STORING SALSA

Allow the flavors of the salsa to mingle before serving for the best flavor; an hour or two is all you need.

- Make just enough salsa at a time to use within a day or two for the freshest flavor and texture.

VARIATIONS ▶

Variations

BACON-CORN SALSA
Cut off the kernels from an ear of cooked corn. Stir corn and 4 to 6 slices crisply cooked and crumbled bacon into prepared salsa.

EASY BRUSCHETTA
Top slices of toasted baguette with spoonfuls of prepared salsa. If you like, toss salsa with prepared olive tapenade before spooning onto baguette slices.

MEXICAN PIZZA
Heat oven to 425°F. Spread your favorite 12-inch pizza crust with ½ cup refried beans. Drizzle with ½ cup canned red enchilada sauce. Sprinkle with ¾ cup shredded Mexican cheese. Bake about 15 minutes or until cheese is bubbly and melted. Top with ½ cup prepared salsa. Garnish with sour cream if desired.

SALSA EGGS
Top cooked eggs (hard-cooked, scrambled, fried or poached) with prepared salsa. Garnish with sliced avocado and sour cream if desired.

SOUTH-OF-THE-BORDER GAZPACHO
In blender, place prepared salsa and ½ cup spicy tomato juice; cover and blend until desired consistency. If you prefer a thinner soup, stir in additional tomato juice. Serve immediately.

HUMMUS WITH PITA CHIPS

16 SERVINGS   PREP TIME: 10 MINUTES   START TO FINISH: 25 MINUTES

HUMMUS

- **1** **can (19 oz) chick peas (garbanzo beans), drained, ¼ cup liquid reserved**
- **½** **cup tahini**
- **¼** **cup extra-virgin olive oil**
- **3** **tablespoons fresh lemon juice**
- **2** **cloves garlic, finely chopped**
- **1** **teaspoon salt**
- **⅛** **teaspoon pepper**
- **Chopped fresh parsley**

PITA CHIPS

- **4** **whole wheat pita (pocket) breads (6 inch)**
- **4** **tablespoons extra-virgin olive oil**
- **½** **teaspoon kosher (coarse) salt**

1. In food processor or blender, place all hummus ingredients except parsley. Cover; blend on high speed, stopping blender occasionally to scrape down sides, until smooth. Spoon hummus into serving dish. Sprinkle with parsley.

2. Heat oven to 375°F. Brush both sides of each pita bread with 1 tablespoon oil. Cut each pita bread into 8 wedges; separate wedges to make 16 wedges for each pita bread. Place wedges on ungreased cookie sheets. Sprinkle with kosher salt.

3. Bake 10 to 12 minutes or until pita chips are crisp and lightly browned. Serve with hummus.

1 SERVING (2 TABLESPOONS HUMMUS AND 4 PITA CHIPS): CALORIES 190; TOTAL FAT 12G (SATURATED FAT 1.5G, TRANS FAT 0G); CHOLESTEROL 0MG; SODIUM 350MG; TOTAL CARBOHYDRATE 17G (DIETARY FIBER 3G); PROTEIN 5G **EXCHANGES:** 1 STARCH, ½ VEGETABLE, 2 FAT **CARBOHYDRATE CHOICES:** 1

Techniques

Hummus is a thick Middle Eastern sauce typically served as a dip with pita chips. It's loved not only for its simplicity and flavor, but also for being a plant-based protein-rich snack.

INGREDIENT FACTS

- Tahini is a paste made from ground sesame seed. It can be found near the international ingredients in many grocery stores or in Middle Eastern markets.
- One-half cup sesame seed can be substituted for the tahini. The hummus just won't be as smooth as if you'd used tahini.
- We call for extra-virgin olive oil for its extra fruity taste, which enhances the hummus's flavor, but you can substitute regular olive oil if you prefer.
- You can use either Italian (flat-leaf) or curly parsley if you prefer. Use whatever you have on hand.
- Serve hummus with cut-up crisp veggies such as bell peppers, broccoli, cauliflower or sliced zucchini or summer squash instead of pita chips.

PEELING GARLIC

- Pull clove away from the garlic bulb (head).
- Cut off stem end of clove.
- Lay the flat side of a wide chef's knife on top of clove. Pound down on knife with fist to lightly smash the garlic (be careful not to touch sharp edge of knife).
- Remove and discard papery layers (which should be easy to remove from the smashed garlic).
- Finely chop or slice garlic as directed in recipe.

CHOPPING PARSLEY

- Hold parsley bunch at an angle on cutting board, with stems up off the board.
- Using a chef's knife, cut away the majority of the stems from leaves.
- Chop the leaf portion of the parsley. (Cut just enough for use; save remaining parsley bunch for another use.) The stems can be used for the hummus or for guacamole, pesto or salsa. Or add to soups, stews or sauces. It can be frozen to have on hand for when you need it.

GREAT HUMMUS DIPPERS

Serve hummus with cut-up crisp veggies such as bell peppers, broccoli, cauliflower or sliced zucchini or summer squash instead of pita chips.

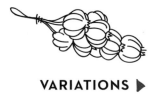

VARIATIONS ▶

Variations

MEDITERRANEAN SANDWICHES
Rather than using the pita bread to make chips, use it for sandwiches instead. Cut pitas in half; open bread to form pockets. Spread 1 tablespoon hummus onto inside top and bottom of each pita half. Fill pita pockets with lettuce, sliced salami or cooked chicken, roasted bell peppers, pitted kalamata olives and crumbled feta cheese.

PESTO-HUMMUS PASTA
Prepare hummus as directed. Stir 2 to 3 tablespoons prepared pesto into ¼ cup prepared hummus. Toss with 4 cups hot cooked pasta. Sprinkle with 2 tablespoons chopped fresh basil or parsley and 2 teaspoons fresh lemon juice; toss again.

SPICY BLACK BEAN HUMMUS
Prepare hummus as directed—except substitute 1 can (19 ounces) black beans for the chick peas and fresh lime juice for the lemon juice. Omit tahini and add 1 can (4.5 ounces) chopped green chiles (undrained) and ½ teaspoon ground cumin with the beans. Serve with pita chips or tortilla chips.

SRIRACHA–ROASTED BELL PEPPER HUMMUS
Prepare hummus as directed—except add ½ cup roasted red bell peppers (from a jar) and ½ to 1 teaspoon Sriracha sauce with the chick peas.

SUN-DRIED TOMATO HUMMUS
Prepare hummus as directed. Stir ¼ cup finely chopped drained sun-dried tomatoes in oil into the prepared hummus for a punch of flavor and color.

BRIE IN PUFF PASTRY
with Cranberry Sauce

12 SERVINGS   PREP TIME: **30 MINUTES**   START TO FINISH: **1 HOUR 25 MINUTES**

CRANBERRY SAUCE*

- **1   cup fresh cranberries**
- **6   tablespoons packed brown sugar**
- **1   tablespoon fresh orange juice**
- **½   teaspoon fresh grated orange zest**

BRIE IN PASTRY

- **1   tablespoon butter**
- **⅓   cup sliced almonds**
- **1   frozen puff pastry sheet (from 17.3-oz package), thawed**
- **1   round (14 to 15 oz) Brie cheese**
- **1   egg, beaten**
- **Assorted crackers or sliced fresh fruit, if desired**

1. In 1-quart saucepan, stir cranberries, brown sugar and orange juice until well mixed. Heat to boiling, stirring frequently; reduce heat. Simmer uncovered 15 to 20 minutes, stirring frequently, until mixture thickens and cranberries are tender. Stir in orange zest; remove from heat.

2. In 8-inch skillet, melt butter over medium heat. Cook almonds in butter, stirring frequently, until golden brown; remove from heat.

3. Heat oven to 400°F. Spray cookie sheet with cooking spray. On lightly floured surface, roll pastry into 16x9-inch rectangle; cut out one 8½-inch round and one 7-inch round.

4. Remove paper from cheese; leave rind on if desired. Place cheese on center of 8½-inch pastry round. Spoon cranberry sauce and almonds over cheese. Bring pastry edge up and press around side of cheese. Brush top edge of pastry with egg. Place 7-inch pastry round on top, pressing around edge to seal. Brush top and side of pastry with egg. Cut decorations from remaining pastry and arrange on top; brush with egg. Place on cookie sheet.

5. Bake 20 to 25 minutes or until golden brown. Cool on cookie sheet on cooling rack 30 minutes before serving. Serve with crackers.

*1 cup purchased whole berry cranberry sauce can be substituted for the cranberry sauce.

1 SERVING: CALORIES 270; TOTAL FAT 19G (SATURATED FAT 9G, TRANS FAT 1G); CHOLESTEROL 75MG; SODIUM 270MG; TOTAL CARBOHYDRATE 17G (DIETARY FIBER 0G); PROTEIN 9G **EXCHANGES:** 1 STARCH, 1 HIGH-FAT MEAT, 2 FAT **CARBOHYDRATE CHOICES:** 1

Techniques

Place Brie on one pastry round. Spread cranberry sauce on Brie.

Bring up pastry edge around Brie. Top with second pastry round.

Brush pastry with beaten egg.

Decorate wrapped pastry round with cutouts from remaining pastry. Brush with beaten egg.

Brie is a soft cheese that comes with a white rind. The rind can be eaten or removed before using, depending on your preference.

REMOVING THE RIND FROM CHEESE
- Remove Brie from wrapper.
- Wrap in plastic wrap.
- Freeze 30 minutes to 3 hours or until cheese is firm.
- Using a chef's knife, cut off a very thin slice from top and bottom of cheese to remove rind; discard rind.
- Cut thin slices from edge of cheese to remove rind; discard rind.

CHOOSING THE OOZE
You can control how much the Brie oozes when cut into by how long you allow the cheese to cool after baking. If you like your cheese to be very runny, decrease the cooling time. If you want the Brie to hold its shape, let it cool longer than 30 minutes before serving.

PUFF PASTRY KNOW-HOW
- Look for puff pastry in the freezer section of your grocery store near the dessert or dough items. Thaw as directed on the package before using.
- Place thawed pastry on a lightly floured surface when rolling it to prevent the pastry from sticking.
- Use an 8½-inch-diameter plate or inverted bowl as a template for cutting a circle from the puff pastry.
- Use a small, sharp knife to cut the pastry.
- Brushing the pastry with beaten egg creates a shiny golden crust when baked and acts like glue to hold the pastry pieces together during baking.

VARIATIONS ▶

Variations

ARTICHOKE-OLIVE BRIE
Prepare Brie as directed—except omit Cranberry Sauce, butter and almonds. In step 4, top Brie with ½ cup chopped marinated artichoke hearts (from 6-oz jar) and 2 tablespoons chopped pimento-stuffed or pitted kalamata olives before wrapping with puff pastry.

BALSAMIC STRAWBERRY BRIE
Prepare Brie as directed—except omit Cranberry Sauce. In step 4, top Brie with ¾ cup sliced fresh strawberries. Drizzle with 3 tablespoons balsamic vinegar. Sprinkle with almonds before wrapping cheese with puff pastry.

FIG AND WALNUT BRIE
Prepare Brie as directed—except omit Cranberry Sauce and substitute chopped walnuts for the almonds. In step 4, spread Brie with ⅓ cup fig preserves. Top with walnuts before wrapping with puff pastry.

PEAR, RASPBERRY AND BACON BRIE
Prepare Brie as directed—except omit Cranberry Sauce, butter and almonds. In step 4, top Brie with 1 ripe pear, thinly sliced (overlapping the slices as necessary), ¾ cup fresh raspberries and 3 slices crisply cooked and crumbled bacon before wrapping with puff pastry.

TOMATO-BASIL BRIE
Prepare Brie as directed—except omit Cranberry Sauce, butter and almonds. In step 4, top Brie with fresh basil leaves and thin tomato slices before wrapping with puff pastry.

SALMON
with Basil Pesto

10 SERVINGS   PREP TIME: **20 MINUTES**   START TO FINISH: **2 HOURS 55 MINUTES**

SALMON

1¼   **lb salmon fillet**

1   **tablespoon fresh lemon juice**

1   **tablespoon olive or vegetable oil**

¼   **teaspoon seasoned salt**

¼   **teaspoon coarsely ground pepper**

BASIL PESTO

2   **cups firmly packed fresh basil leaves**

¾   **cup grated Parmesan cheese**

½   **cup olive or vegetable oil**

¼   **cup pine nuts, toasted if desired**

3   **cloves garlic, peeled**

SERVE-WITHS

Lemon wedges or spirals, if desired

Fresh basil leaves, if desired

40   **slices cocktail bread**

1. Heat oven to 400°F. Spray shallow baking pan with cooking spray. Place salmon in pan. Brush with lemon juice and oil. Sprinkle with seasoned salt and pepper. Bake 15 to 20 minutes or until fish flakes easily with fork.

2. Remove salmon from pan. Cool about 15 minutes. Cover and refrigerate at least 2 hours but no longer than 24 hours.

3. Meanwhile, make basil pesto. In food processor or blender, place all ingredients. Cover and process on medium speed about 3 minutes, stopping occasionally to scrape down sides with rubber spatula, until smooth.

4. Place salmon, skin side down, on serving platter. (Carefully remove skin if desired.) Spoon 1 to 2 tablespoons pesto over salmon. Place remaining pesto in small serving bowl. Garnish salmon with basil leaves and lemon wedges. Serve with cocktail bread.

1 SERVING (2 OZ SALMON, 2 TABLESPOONS PESTO AND 4 SLICES COCKTAIL BREAD): CALORIES 340; TOTAL FAT 24G (SATURATED FAT 4.5G, TRANS FAT 0G); CHOLESTEROL 40MG; SODIUM 350MG; TOTAL CARBOHYDRATE 15G (DIETARY FIBER 1G); PROTEIN 17G **EXCHANGES:** 1 STARCH, 2 LEAN MEAT, 3½ FAT **CARBOHYDRATE CHOICES:** 1

See Cooking Fish (page 109) for how to tell when fish is done.

MAKING PESTO

Pesto is an uncooked sauce typically made with fresh basil, garlic, Parmesan cheese, olive oil and pine nuts. This easy sauce takes just minutes to make and adds a terrific flavor punch typically to pasta but can be used in lots of other ways as well (see below).

- Use just the leaves (no stems) of fresh basil, being sure to pack them firmly in the measuring cup to get an accurate measurement.
- If using other herbs that have tender stems, such as cilantro or parsley, the stems can be used as well as the leaves.
- Pesto can be customized by varying the ingredients. Swap in other herbs or greens for the basil, or use a combination of greens and herbs. Change the nuts, or make a nut-free pesto by leaving them out (the pesto may be a little more runny).
- Toasting nuts adds another layer of flavor. To toast the pine nuts, sprinkle them in an ungreased skillet. Cook over medium heat 5 to 7 minutes, stirring frequently until they begin to brown, then stir constantly until golden brown.

OTHER USES FOR PESTO

Pesto is typically used as a sauce for pasta, but it's also great for a host of other uses. Experiment with these ways to use it or come up with your own:

- Spread over other fish (such as cod, snapper or tilapia), shrimp or scallops before cooking, or dollop onto cooked fish or shrimp before serving.
- Use instead of pizza sauce on pizza.
- Stir some into the deviled egg mixture before spooning into the eggs.
- Spread a little on sandwiches instead of mayonnaise or mustard.
- Stir a small amount into scrambled eggs before cooking, or spoon on top of cooked eggs.
- Spread on slices of French bread, top with shredded mozzarella cheese and broil to make cheesy bread.

VARIATIONS ▶

SALMON WITH BASIL PESTO (CONTINUED)

Variations

BASIL, ROASTED RED PEPPER AND WALNUT PESTO
Prepare Basil Pesto as directed—except use food processor. Decrease basil to 1 cup and oil to ⅓ cup. Add ½ cup drained roasted red or yellow bell peppers (from a jar). Substitute walnuts for the pine nuts.

CILANTRO PESTO
Prepare Basil Pesto as directed—except substitute 1½ cups firmly packed fresh cilantro and ½ cup firmly packed fresh parsley for the basil.

GREEK SALMON WITH BASIL PESTO
Prepare as directed—except spoon all of the pesto onto fish. Sprinkle with ¼ cup each pitted kalamata olives, chopped drained roasted red pepper (from a jar) and feta cheese. Omit basil sprigs and lemon wedges.

SHRIMP AND FETTUCCINE WITH BASIL PESTO
Omit salmon and serve-withs. Prepare Basil Pesto as directed. Toss 1 pound cooked and drained fettuccine with ½ cup pesto (add more if desired). Add 1 package (12 ounces) thawed (deveined and tails removed) frozen medium cooked shrimp. Sprinkle with grated Parmesan cheese and pepper before serving. Serve as a main dish or first course.

SUN-DRIED TOMATO PESTO
Prepare Basil Pesto as directed—except use food processor. Omit basil. Decrease oil to ⅓ cup. Add ½ cup sun-dried tomatoes in oil, undrained.

Italian
STUFFED MUSHROOMS

3 DOZEN MUSHROOMS   PREP TIME: **20 MINUTES**   START TO FINISH: **35 MINUTES**

36   **medium whole fresh mushrooms (1 lb)**

3   **tablespoons butter**

¼   **cup chopped green onions (4 medium)**

¼   **cup chopped red bell pepper**

1½   **cups soft bread crumbs**

2   **teaspoons Italian seasoning**

¼   **teaspoon salt**

¼   **teaspoon pepper**

Grated Parmesan cheese, if desired

1. Heat oven to 350°F. Twist mushroom stems to remove from mushroom caps. Finely chop enough stems to measure ⅓ cup. Reserve mushroom caps.

2. In 10-inch skillet, melt 2 tablespoons of the butter over medium-high heat. Cook chopped mushroom stems, onions and bell pepper in butter about 3 minutes, stirring frequently, until onions are softened; remove from heat. Stir in bread crumbs, Italian seasoning, salt and pepper. Fill mushroom caps with bread crumb mixture.

3. Melt remaining 1 tablespoon butter in 13x9-inch baking pan in oven. Place mushrooms filled side up in pan. Sprinkle with cheese. Bake 15 minutes.

4. Set oven control to Broil. Broil mushrooms with tops 3 to 4 inches from heat about 2 minutes or until tops are light brown. Serve hot.

1 MUSHROOM: CALORIES 30; TOTAL FAT 1G (SATURATED FAT 0.5G, TRANS FAT 0G); CHOLESTEROL 0MG; SODIUM 60MG; TOTAL CARBOHYDRATE 4G (DIETARY FIBER 0G); PROTEIN 1G **EXCHANGES:** ½ STARCH **CARBOHYDRATE CHOICES:** 0

Techniques

WORKING WITH MUSHROOMS

Stuffed mushrooms are an always-sought-after appetizer at any occasion, so it's a great recipe to have in your repertoire. They are easy to make if you know a few tricks:

- Fresh mushrooms will have firm caps with good color and no soft spots or decay. Wash mushrooms just before using; pat dry if wet.
- We use some of the mushroom stems as part of the bread crumb mixture. Don't add them all, or you'll have too much filling for the mushroom caps left over. Add remaining stems to egg dishes, soups or casseroles.
- The filling can be cooked quickly if you have all the ingredients prepped before you start cooking.
- Use a small ice-cream scoop or the large end of a melon ball cutter to scoop the vegetable mixture evenly into the mushroom caps.
- Prep the mushrooms ahead of your event and then bake them right before your guests arrive. Stuff, cover and refrigerate the mushrooms up to 24 hours ahead. Then when you're ready for hot appetizers, simply start with step 4.

VARIATIONS ▶

Variations

BACON AND PARMESAN STUFFED MUSHROOMS
Prepare as directed—except omit bell pepper. Substitute chopped fresh parsley for the Italian seasoning and decrease bread crumbs to 1¼ cups. Add 8 slices crisply cooked and crumbled bacon and ½ cup grated Parmesan cheese with the bread crumbs.

GORGONZOLA AND HAZELNUT STUFFED MUSHROOMS
Prepare as directed—except chop enough mushroom stems to equal ½ cup. Omit soft bread crumbs, Italian seasoning and Parmesan cheese. Increase salt to ½ teaspoon. Stir ⅓ cup crumbled Gorgonzola cheese, ½ cup seasoned bread crumbs, ¼ cup chopped hazelnuts (filberts), the salt and pepper into mushroom mixture.

JALAPEÑO POPPER STUFFED MUSHROOMS
Prepare as directed—except substitute 1 can (7 ounces) drained chopped green chiles for the green onions, 2 tablespoons chopped fresh cilantro for the Italian seasoning and 3 tablespoons shredded Cheddar cheese for the Parmesan cheese.

SAUSAGE STUFFED MUSHROOMS
Prepare as directed—except substitute chopped onion for the green onions and omit red bell pepper. Reduce butter to 1 tablespoon and bread crumbs to ¼ cup. Add 1 pound bulk pork sausage, 2 tablespoons chopped fresh chives, 1 finely chopped clove garlic and ¼ cup grated Parmesan cheese. In 10-inch skillet, cook sausage, chopped mushroom stems, chives, onion and garlic until sausage is no longer pink; drain. Stir bread crumbs and ¼ cup Parmesan cheese into sausage mixture until mixture holds together. Continue as directed in step 3.

SPINACH AND SUN-DRIED TOMATO STUFFED MUSHROOMS:
Prepare as directed—except substitute ¼ cup frozen (thawed) spinach squeezed to remove moisture (from 10-ounce package) for the green onions and ¼ cup drained chopped sun-dried tomatoes in oil for the red bell pepper. Omit Italian seasoning. Stir Parmesan cheese into the mixture before filling mushroom caps. Sprinkle additional Parmesan cheese over filling before baking.

Throw Together an AMAZING CHARCUTERIE BOARD

This incredibly easy appetizer is a breeze to put together and will impress your guests at the same time. Choose an item or two from each category and then get the party started!

CURED MEATS AND CHEESES

Select cured meats and cheeses that range in flavor from mild to bold as well as cheeses with a variety of textures.

BREAD AND CRACKERS

Offer something soft and chewy, such as slices of baguette, and a crisp or crunchy option like breadsticks or crackers.

BRINED AND SPICY

Brined foods such as pickles or olives pair well with the meat and cheese. Spicy foods are available in nearly every category such as spicy almonds and jalapeño jam, both of which add layers of flavor.

CONDIMENTS

Sweet jams, preserves or chutney balance out the dry, salty meats and cheeses. Mustard, tapenade, pâté or hummus are also great choices.

NUTS FOR CRUNCH

Tucked into small spaces between the other foods, nuts add visual and textural interest to your display.

Caramelized Onion, Nectarine and Bacon FLATBREADS

12 SLICES   PREP TIME: **40 MINUTES**   START TO FINISH: **1 HOUR**

Pizza Crust (page 60)

CARAMELIZED ONIONS

- **2 tablespoons butter**
- **2 large sweet onions or yellow onions, sliced (4 cups)**
- **2 teaspoons chopped fresh thyme or ½ teaspoon dried thyme**
- **¼ teaspoon salt**
- **¼ teaspoon pepper**

TOPPING

- **1 container (8 oz) soft spreadable cream cheese**
- **2 oz crumbled goat or blue cheese**
- **1 ripe nectarine, pitted, thinly sliced**
- **2 tablespoons crisply cooked and crumbled bacon**
- **Chopped fresh thyme**

1. Make pizza crust as directed in recipe—except after resting, divide dough into 3 equal portions. Reserve 1 portion for another use.*

2. Meanwhile, in 12-inch nonstick skillet, melt butter over medium-high heat. Stir in onions, thyme, salt and pepper. Cook uncovered 15 to 20 minutes, stirring frequently, until deep golden brown.

3. Heat oven to 425°F. Line large cookie sheet with parchment paper. Pat each dough portion into 12x6-inch rectangle. Place dough rectangles on pan about 2 inches apart. Prick dough with fork every few inches to prevent air bubbles. Bake 9 to 11 minutes or until crust is golden brown. Cool 5 minutes.

4. Spread cream cheese onto each crust to within ½ inch of edge. Sprinkle evenly with goat cheese. Arrange onions and nectarine slices evenly over cheese. Sprinkle with bacon and thyme.

5. Bake 4 to 5 minutes longer or until topping is heated through. Cut each flatbread crosswise into 6 slices.

*The extra portion of dough can be shaped and baked as directed for the flatbread. After cooling, place in a resealable freezer plastic bag, removing all air. Freeze up to 2 to 3 months. Thaw at room temperature, and use for Pesto Caprese Flatbread or with another topping of your choice for a quick appetizer anytime.

1 SLICE: CALORIES 200; TOTAL FAT 12G (SATURATED FAT 6G, TRANS FAT 0G); CHOLESTEROL 25MG; SODIUM 310MG; TOTAL CARBOHYDRATE 20G (DIETARY FIBER 1G); PROTEIN 5G **EXCHANGES:** ½ STARCH, 1 OTHER CARBOHYDRATE, ½ LEAN MEAT, 2 FAT **CARBOHYDRATE CHOICES:** 1

MAKING PIZZA CRUST
See Making Pizza Crust (page 61).

CARAMELIZED ONION TIPS
Caramelized onions are a great addition to many dishes. Their rich flavor is hard to beat. Many think caramelized onions are hard to make, but they aren't if you know a few tips:

- Sweet onions such as Bermuda, Maui, Vidalia and Walla Walla have more sugar than regular onions. It's the sugar in the onions that caramelizes, giving them the dark color and depth of flavor. If you use yellow onions instead of sweet onions, sprinkle them in the pan with a tablespoon of brown sugar before cooking.
- Slice onions about ¼ inch thick so they can cook slowly and caramelize. If sliced too thin, the onions will burn rather than caramelize. Thicker slices will take longer to caramelize.
- Butter is better than oil to get the rich, characteristic flavor of good caramelized onions.
- Use a nonstick skillet to avoid the onions sticking to the pan and burning. This allows you to cook the onions at medium-high heat, which isn't too hot to burn the onions or too low to require 30 minutes or more to cook them.
- Be sure to use a 12-inch pan so that the onions aren't crowded. They will cook more quickly and evenly if not crowded.

OTHER USES FOR CARAMELIZED ONIONS
Caramelized onions are great on so many foods. Add them to any of these for a special treat:

- Burgers
- Panini sandwiches
- Pizza
- Scrambled eggs
- Egg bakes
- Cooked green beans

VARIATIONS ▶

Variations

CARAMELIZED ONION AND BLUEBERRY FLATBREAD
Prepare as directed—except substitute about 1 cup fresh blueberries for the nectarine. Omit bacon.

CARAMELIZED ONION, APPLE AND PROSCIUTTO FLATBREAD
Prepare as directed—except substitute thinly sliced unpeeled apple for the nectarine and chopped prosciutto for the crisply cooked and crumbled bacon.

CARAMELIZED ONION, CHICKEN AND PESTO FLATBREAD
Prepare as directed—except substitute ¼ cup pesto (page 36 or 39 or prepared pesto) for the goat cheese. Top each of the flatbreads with ½ cup finely chopped cooked chicken before adding the caramelized onions. Omit nectarine, bacon and thyme.

CARAMELIZED ONION, CRANBERRY AND POMEGRANATE FLATBREAD
Prepare as directed—except spoon ⅔ cup whole cranberry sauce over cheeses. After topping flatbreads with caramelized onions, top with ¼ cup fresh pomegranate seeds and bacon. Omit nectarine and thyme.

CARAMELIZED ONIONS WITH GRAPE OR PEAR FLATBREAD
Prepare as directed—except substitute 1 cup green or red seedless grape halves or 1 sliced ripe pear (any variety) for the nectarine.

BRUSCHETTA

12 SERVINGS   PREP TIME: **20 MINUTES**   START TO FINISH: **20 MINUTES**

12 slices Italian bread, ½ inch thick

¼ cup olive or vegetable oil

2 medium tomatoes, chopped (1½ cups)

2 cloves garlic, finely chopped

3 tablespoons chopped fresh basil leaves

2 tablespoons small capers, drained

½ teaspoon salt

½ teaspoon pepper

1. Place bread slices on ungreased cookie sheet. Drizzle 1 teaspoon oil over each slice. Set oven control to broil. Broil with tops 4 inches from heat 1 to 2 minutes or until lightly browned. Turn bread; broil 1 to 2 minutes longer or until lightly browned.

2. Mix remaining ingredients. Spoon tomato mixture onto bread slices. Serve at room temperature.

1 SERVING (1 SLICE BREAD AND 2 TABLESPOONS TOPPING): CALORIES 100; TOTAL FAT 5G (SATURATED FAT 0.5G, TRANS FAT 0G); CHOLESTEROL 0MG; SODIUM 240MG; TOTAL CARBOHYDRATE 11G (DIETARY FIBER 1G); PROTEIN 2G **EXCHANGES:** ½ STARCH, 1 FAT **CARBOHYDRATE CHOICES:** 1

TEST KITCHEN TIP

You can use whatever savory buns or rolls you have on hand for the Italian bread, if you wish. Cut rolls horizontally in half. You may need more pieces to hold all the topping, if they are small.

Techniques

Pronounced "broo-SHEH-tah" and meaning "to roast over coals," bruschetta is a traditional Italian garlic bread that's drizzled with olive oil.

Bruschetta is one of our favorite finger foods. It's an easy appetizer that requires just 10 minutes of prep and packs big flavor. Bruschetta is an appetizer you need at your next party!

CAPERS

Capers are the fruit of the caper bush. Some are not much larger than the end of a cotton swab; others are twice that size. After harvesting, they are packed in brine. Look for them in the pickle aisle.

Just give them a whack with the side of a chef's knife before adding them to your recipe to release more flavor, if you wish.

BROILING

When broiling, the food is cooked a short distance from a direct heat source. This technique can be completed in a gas or electric oven. The broiler will be located in the oven or sometimes in a compartment under the oven.

Some think of broiling as a cousin to grilling because the surfaces of food are well browned, creating a wonderful caramelized taste. Advantages of broiling include quickly cooked foods with great flavor and minimal cleanup.

To determine the distance between the food and the broiler pan, place the pan in a cold oven. Then measure the distance from where the food will be to the broiler element. Use the distance recommended in the recipe you are using, or refer to the oven manufacturer's recommendations. Always watch food carefully while broiling to prevent burning.

BROILING TIPS

- Turn the broiler on 5 to 10 minutes ahead of time so that it can heat up.
- For easy cleanup, line the broiler pan with foil and poke holes through to let the juices drain. The bottom pan can also be lined with foil.
- Place the food in the center of the pan.
- Place the pan under the broiler at the distance indicated in the recipe (see above).
- On most ovens, you can leave the oven door open slightly to allow air to circulate. This also helps to keep steam from forming in the oven—too much steam and the food will not have a crisp crust. But check the oven manufacturer's guidelines to be sure this is recommended.
- Remove the pan from the oven to turn the food as indicated in the recipe directions.
- Follow recipe times carefully. If food is not quite cooked, you can place it under the broiler for a bit longer.

VARIATIONS ▶

BRUSCHETTA (CONTINUED)

Variations

APPLE, FONTINA AND PISTACHIO BRUSCHETTA
Prepare as directed—except omit toppings. Top each broiled bread slice with 1 small piece fontina cheese (about 4½ ounces), and sprinkle with 2 tablespoons fchopped shelled pistachios. Broil about 1 minute or just until cheese is melted. Top with 1 thin slice of apple; press lightly into cheese.

ARTICHOKE-PARMESAN BRUSCHETTA
Prepare as directed—except omit step 2. Spread each bread slice with about 1 tablespoon prepared artichoke dip. Sprinkle with shredded or shaved Asiago or Parmesan cheese. Serve as is, or broil about 1 minute or just until cheese is melted.

BEEF TENDERLOIN BRUSCHETTA
Prepare as directed—except omit step 2. Spread each bread slice with about 2 teaspoons chive-and-onion cream cheese spread. Top with thinly sliced cooked beef tenderloin or roast beef, thinly sliced or chopped plum (Roma) tomato and chopped fresh parsley.

BLACK BEAN AND COTIJA BRUSCHETTA
Prepare as directed—except omit step 2. Spread each bread slice with about 1 tablespoon purchased black bean dip or refried black beans. Top with 1 heaping teaspoon of salsa. Sprinkle with crumbled cotija (white Mexican) or shredded Cheddar cheese and whole or chopped fresh cilantro leaves. Or substitute guacamole for the dip or refried beans.

BRIE, RASPBERRY AND PEAR BRUSCHETTA
Prepare as directed—except omit step 2. Lightly spread each bread slice with about 2 teaspoons seedless raspberry preserves. Top with thinly sliced pear and thin slices of Brie cheese. Broil about 1 minute or just until cheese is melted.

POLENTA NUGGETS
with Sriracha Dipping Sauce

8 SERVINGS   PREP TIME: **20 MINUTES**   START TO FINISH: **1 HOUR 20 MINUTES**

POLENTA

- **1 cup yellow cornmeal**
- **3¼ cups water**
- **1 teaspoon salt**
- **1 cup finely shredded Parmesan cheese**

SRIRACHA DIPPING SAUCE

- **½ cup sour cream**
- **2 tablespoons chopped green onions (2 medium)**
- **2 tablespoons chopped roasted red pepper (from 12-oz jar)**
- **2 teaspoons Sriracha sauce**
- **Additional chopped green onion, if desired**

1. Spray 8-inch square (2-quart) glass baking dish with cooking spray.

2. In heavy 3-quart saucepan, mix cornmeal and ¾ cup water. Stir in remaining 2½ cups water and the salt. Cook over medium heat 8 to 10 minutes, stirring constantly, until mixture thickens and boils; reduce heat.

3. Cover; simmer about 10 minutes, stirring occasionally, until very thick. Remove from heat; stir in cheese. Spread mixture evenly in baking dish. Refrigerate uncovered 45 minutes or until set. (To make up to 1 day ahead, cover when set and refrigerate.)

4. Meanwhile, in small bowl, combine dipping sauce ingredients except additional green onion; mix well. Sprinkle with additional green onion. Cover and refrigerate until serving time.

5. Heat broiler. Line large baking sheet with foil, and spray with cooking spray or brush with oil. (Uncover polenta if made ahead and lightly blot any water on top of polenta with a paper towel.) Unmold polenta onto cutting board. Cut into 8 rows by 4 rows. Arrange polenta nuggets in single layer at least ½ inch apart on pan. Spray with cooking spray.

6. Broil 4 inches from heat 10 to 15 minutes, turning once during broiling and rearranging nuggets on pan if browning unevenly, until golden. Immediately remove nuggets from pan to cooling rack. Serve warm with dipping sauce.

1 SERVING (4 NUGGETS AND 1 TABLESPOON DIPPING SAUCE): CALORIES 160; TOTAL FAT 7G (SATURATED FAT 4G, TRANS FAT 0G); CHOLESTEROL 20MG; SODIUM 530MG; TOTAL CARBOHYDRATE 17G (DIETARY FIBER 1G); PROTEIN 7G **EXCHANGES:** 1 STARCH, ½ LEAN MEAT, 1 FAT **CARBOHYDRATE CHOICES:** 1

Techniques

WHAT IS POLENTA?

A staple in Northern Italy and Eastern European countries, Southerners know this dish as cornmeal mush. It's yellow cornmeal cooked with water, salt and butter similarly to oatmeal.

Polenta is very versatile, showing up for breakfast, served hot with maple syrup, or cooled and fried as a side dish served with pasta sauce.

We've paired it with Sriracha Dipping Sauce, but it would also be great dipped in salsa, pasta sauce, ranch dressing or barbecue sauce.

TIPS FOR MAKING POLENTA

- Medium- to coarse-grain cornmeal or polenta may require longer cooking.
- Prevent the cornmeal from clumping when combining it with the water by adding only some of the water at first as in step 2. Once that is mixed, it's easier to add the remaining water.
- Use the pan size called for in the recipe and cook over medium heat so that the cornmeal can cook as long as it needs to, absorbing the water at an even rate. This ensures that the polenta will be neither runny nor lumpy.
- Polenta will be very thick and may bubble when cooking. Use a long-handled spoon to safely stir the mixture while cooking.

VARIATIONS ▶

Variations

BACON-CHEDDAR POLENTA NUGGETS
Prepare as directed—except substitute 1 cup finely shredded Cheddar cheese for the Parmesan cheese, and add ½ cup crisply cooked and finely chopped bacon with the cheese.

CAPRESE POLENTA NUGGETS
Prepare as directed. Top each nugget with a small fresh basil leaf, a slice of plum (Roma) tomato and a pearl-size fresh mozzarella ball; secure with decorative pick. Serve with Basil Pesto (page 36), if desired.

CHIVE-PEPPER POLENTA NUGGETS
Prepare as directed—except stir in ¼ cup chopped fresh chives and ½ teaspoon pepper with the cornmeal.

POLENTA CUPS
Prepare polenta as directed—except do not stir in the cheese. Omit Sriracha Dipping Sauce. Spray 36 mini muffin cups with cooking spray. Spoon polenta evenly into cups, filling each about three-quarters full. With back of spoon dipped in cold water, gently form indentation in center of each cup. Refrigerate uncovered 30 minutes. Remove from pan. Fill cups with toppings such as Bruschetta Topping (page 50), Fresh Tomato Salsa (page 24), Guacamole (page 20), or Caramelized Onions (page 46) and crisply cooked and crumbled bacon. Heat filled or unfilled cups at 350°F about 5 minutes or until hot.

POLENTA NUGGETS WITH BASIL PESTO
Prepare as directed—except substitute Basil Pesto (page 36) for the Sriracha Dipping Sauce.

UNFORGETTABLE

Mains

legendary
CHICKEN TACO PIZZA

8 SERVINGS   PREP TIME: **45 MINUTES**   START TO FINISH: **1 HOUR 35 MINUTES**

PIZZA CRUST

2½ to 3	**cups all-purpose, bread or whole wheat flour**
1	**tablespoon sugar**
1	**teaspoon salt**
1	**package (2¼ teaspoons) regular active or fast-acting dry yeast**
1	**cup very warm water (120°F to 130°F)**
3	**tablespoons olive or vegetable oil**
2	**teaspoons cornmeal**

PIZZA TOPPINGS

1	**cup refried beans**
1	**cup thick and chunky salsa**
2	**cups chopped cooked chicken**
1½	**cups shredded Cheddar cheese (6 oz)**
4	**cups shredded lettuce**
1	**small tomato, chopped**
1	**avocado, peeled, cut into slices**
	Taco sauce or salsa, if desired

1. In large bowl, mix 1 cup flour, the sugar, salt and yeast. Add water and oil. Beat with electric mixer on medium speed 3 minutes, scraping bowl frequently. Stir in enough remaining flour until dough is soft and leaves side of bowl. Place dough on lightly floured surface; knead about 5 minutes or until dough is smooth and springy.

2. Cover loosely with plastic wrap and let rest 30 minutes.

3. Heat oven to 425°F. Follow directions for desired crust (see Shaping and Prebaking Pizza Dough at right).

4. Spoon refried beans evenly over each pizza crust. Spoon salsa, chicken and cheese evenly over crusts. Bake as directed for desired crust or until cheese is melted. Before serving, top with lettuce, tomato and avocado. Drizzle with taco sauce. Cut into 8 wedges each.

1 SERVING (2 SLICES): CALORIES 420; TOTAL FAT 18G (SATURATED FAT 6G, TRANS FAT 0G); CHOLESTEROL 50MG; SODIUM 810MG; TOTAL CARBOHYDRATE 42G (DIETARY FIBER 5G); PROTEIN 21G **EXCHANGES:** 1 STARCH, 2 OTHER CARBOHYDRATE, 2 VERY LEAN MEAT, ½ HIGH-FAT MEAT, 2½ FAT **CARBOHYDRATE CHOICES:** 3

Techniques

MAKING PIZZA CRUST

See Measuring Ingredients (page 195).
See Working with Yeast (page 199).
See Kneading Yeast Dough (page 203).

MAKE-AHEAD PIZZA DOUGH

TO REFRIGERATE: After step 2, place dough in greased bowl; tightly cover with plastic wrap and refrigerate up to 4 days. Continue as directed in step 3.

TO FREEZE: After step 2, shape into 2 balls. Wrap each ball tightly in plastic wrap. Freeze up to 2 months. To use, remove from freezer and place in refrigerator until thawed, 4 to 6 hours. Continue as directed in step 3.

SHAPING AND PREBAKING PIZZA DOUGH

For thin crusts: Grease cookie sheet or pizza pan with oil. Sprinkle with cornmeal. Divide dough in half. Pat each half into 12-inch round on cookie sheet using floured fingers. Partially bake 7 to 8 minutes or until crust just begins to brown.

For thick crusts: Grease 2 (8-inch square or 9-inch round) baking pans with oil. Sprinkle with cornmeal. Divide dough in half. Pat each half into bottom of pan using floured fingers.

Cover loosely with plastic wrap; let rise in warm place 30 to 45 minutes or until almost doubled in size.

Move oven rack to lowest position. Heat oven to 375°F. Partially bake 20 to 22 minutes or until crust begins to brown.

VARIATIONS ▶

Variations

BARBECUE PIZZA
Prepare pizzas as directed—except omit toppings. Mix 5 cups shredded cooked chicken or turkey and 2 cups barbecue sauce; spread evenly over each pizza. Top each pizza with ⅓ cup shredded red onion and 1 cup shredded Cheddar cheese. Bake as directed.

CHICKEN RANCH PIZZA
Prepare pizzas as directed—except substitute ranch salad dressing for the refried beans. Omit salsa, lettuce, tomato and avocado.

5-CHEESE PIZZA
Prepare pizzas as directed—except substitute pizza sauce for the refried beans. Omit other toppings. Top each crust with 1 bag (8 ounces) shredded 5-cheese blend. Bake as directed.

MEDITERRANEAN PIZZA
Prepare pizzas as directed—except substitute hummus for refried beans. Omit other toppings. Top each crust with 1 cup shredded zucchini, squeezed to remove excess moisture, ¼ cup chopped bell pepper, ¼ cup sliced kalamata or ripe olives and 2 ounces goat cheese, crumbled. Bake as directed.

SAUSAGE AND KALE PIZZA
Prepare pizzas as directed—except omit toppings. In 10-inch skillet, cook ½ pound bulk Italian sausage, 1 cup sliced mushrooms and ½ cup sliced onion until pork is no longer pink; drain, if necessary, and return to skillet. Stir in 2 cups chopped kale leaves; cook and stir until wilted, 2 to 3 minutes. Spoon ½ cup pizza sauce over each crust. Spread pork and vegetable mixture evenly over each pizza. Sprinkle each pizza with 1 cup mozzarella cheese. Bake as directed.

Company-Worthy
ROASTED CHICKEN AND VEGETABLES

6 SERVINGS   PREP TIME: **30 MINUTES**   START TO FINISH: **2 HOURS 30 MINUTES**

1 whole chicken (4½ to 5 lb)

3 tablespoons olive oil

2 tablespoons chopped fresh rosemary or thyme

1 teaspoon salt

1 teaspoon grated lemon zest

½ teaspoon pepper

1 bulb garlic, divided into cloves, peeled

1 lemon, cut into quarters

1 lb fingerling potatoes, cut lengthwise in half

4 medium carrots, cut into 1-inch chunks

2 large stalks celery, cut into 1-inch chunks

1 large onion, cut into wedges

1. Heat oven to 425°F. Discard giblets and remove excess fat from chicken. Place chicken on rack in shallow roasting pan.

2. In small bowl, stir together oil, rosemary, salt, lemon zest and pepper. Rub cavity and outside of chicken with half of the rosemary mixture. Place 6 cloves garlic and the lemon quarters in cavity of chicken. Tie drumsticks to the tail with kitchen string, if desired.

3. In large bowl, stir potatoes, carrots, celery, onion, remaining garlic and remaining rosemary mixture until vegetables are coated. Arrange vegetables around chicken. Insert ovenproof meat thermometer so tip is in thickest part of inside thigh and does not touch bone. Roast 1 hour 30 minutes to 1 hour 45 minutes or until thermometer reads 165°F and legs move easily when lifted or twisted. Cover loosely with foil; let stand 10 to 15 minutes. Carve chicken; place on platter with vegetables.

1 SERVING: CALORIES 510; TOTAL FAT 27G (SATURATED FAT 7G, TRANS FAT 0.5G); CHOLESTEROL 130MG; SODIUM 570MG; TOTAL CARBOHYDRATE 23G (DIETARY FIBER 3G); PROTEIN 43G **EXCHANGES:** 1 STARCH, 1½ VEGETABLE, 5 VERY LEAN MEAT, 5 FAT **CARBOHYDRATE CHOICES:** 1½

Techniques

PREPARING CHICKEN (OR TURKEY) FOR ROASTING

These tips work for roasting both chicken and turkey.

Adding the garlic and lemons to the cavity adds a lot of flavor while the chicken roasts.

Tying the legs together helps keep the lemons and garlic inside the chicken and gives it a nice shape when roasting.

Rubbing oil and seasonings in cavity and over chicken will help the skin to brown nicely, keep the skin moist and add flavor.

Insert an ovenproof meat thermometer so tip is in thickest part of thigh and does not touch bone.

CARVING CHICKEN (OR TURKEY)

These directions work for carving both whole chicken and whole turkey.

Place chicken, breast side up, on cutting board.

While holding drumstick, cut through joint between thigh and body. Separate drumstick and thigh by cutting through connecting joint.

Remove wings from body by cutting through wing joints.

Just to each side of the breast bone, cut down through meat to remove; slice breast meat.

Variations

HERB-ROASTED CHICKEN AND VEGETABLES

Prepare as directed—except add 1 teaspoon each chopped fresh thyme, sage and oregano leaves with the rosemary and omit garlic. Brush outside of chicken with one third of the herb mixture (do not brush cavity). Place 2 sprigs fresh rosemary and 1 sprig each fresh thyme, sage and oregano in cavity with lemons. Toss remaining herb mixture with vegetables as directed in step 3.

MAPLE-GLAZED THYME-ROASTED CHICKEN AND VEGETABLES

Prepare as directed—except omit rosemary, lemon, lemon zest and garlic. In small bowl, stir together oil, 2 tablespoons chopped fresh thyme leaves, the salt, pepper and ½ teaspoon ground allspice. Continue as directed. Twenty minutes before chicken and vegetables are done, mix 1 tablespoon melted butter with 2 tablespoons real maple syrup; brush over chicken and vegetables. Brush again before chicken is completely cooked.

ORANGE-ROSEMARY ROAST CHICKEN AND VEGETABLES

Prepare as directed—except substitute a quartered orange for the lemon and orange zest for the lemon zest.

PROVENÇAL ROAST CHICKEN

Prepare as directed—except substitute 1 tablespoon dried herbes de Provence for the rosemary. Substitute 8 small quartered red potatoes (1½ pounds); 2 medium zucchini cut into 1½-inch pieces; 1 can (14.5 ounces) drained diced tomatoes with basil, garlic and oregano; and ½ cup chopped pitted kalamata olives for the fingerling potatoes, carrots, celery and onion.

CHICKEN GRAVY

Prepare as directed. After removing chicken and vegetables from pan, scrape all brown particles from pan and pour particles and drippings into bowl or glass measuring cup. Skim 2 tablespoons of fat from the top of the drippings; add fat to 1-quart saucepan. Discard any remaining fat; reserve remaining drippings. Stir 2 tablespoons all-purpose flour into fat in saucepan. Cook over low heat, stirring constantly, 1 to 2 minutes until mixture thickens; remove from heat. Gradually stir in reserved drippings plus enough chicken broth or water to equal 1 cup. Heat to boiling, stirring constantly. Boil and stir 1 minute.

CHICKEN NOODLE SOUP

6 SERVINGS   PREP TIME: **25 MINUTES**   START TO FINISH: **50 MINUTES**

5½ cups Slow-Cooker Chicken Bone Broth (see right) or chicken broth

¼ cup butter

1 cup sliced celery

3 medium carrots, sliced (1½ cups)

1 medium leek, rinsed, cut in half lengthwise and chopped (1 cup)

2 cloves garlic, finely chopped

4½ cups chopped rotisserie chicken (from Slow-Cooker Chicken Bone Broth)

1 teaspoon salt

1 teaspoon chopped fresh thyme or ½ teaspoon dried thyme leaves

½ teaspoon pepper

1 bag (12 oz) frozen egg noodles

1. Prepare Slow-Cooker Chicken Bone Broth, reserving 5½ cups broth and 4½ cups chicken for the soup. Cover and refrigerate any remaining broth and chicken for another use.

2. In 5- to 6-quart Dutch oven or stockpot, melt butter over medium heat. Add celery, carrots, leeks and garlic and cook 3 to 4 minutes, stirring frequently, until crisp-tender. Add remaining ingredients except noodles. Heat to boiling. Reduce heat to low; cook 5 minutes longer.

3. Stir in noodles. Cook uncovered 10 to 15 minutes or until noodles and vegetables are tender.

1 SERVING (1½ CUPS): CALORIES 500; TOTAL FAT 20G (SATURATED FAT 9G, TRANS FAT 0.5G); CHOLESTEROL 180MG; SODIUM 1320MG; TOTAL CARBOHYDRATE 39G (DIETARY FIBER 2G); PROTEIN 41G **EXCHANGES:** 2 STARCH, ½ OTHER CARBOHYDRATE, ½ VEGETABLE, 4½ VERY LEAN MEAT, 3½ FAT **CARBOHYDRATE CHOICES:** 2½

TEST KITCHEN TIP

Cut carrots all the same size to be sure they will all be done when you pierce them with a fork. Test a few pieces to be sure they are all done.

Techniques

MAKING BONE BROTH

Why make bone broth rather than using regular chicken broth? Besides being very economical, the minerals from the bones are released into the broth, boosting the nutritional value of the broth.

- Starting completely from scratch would require roasting the bones before making this slow-simmering broth. By starting with rotisserie chickens, you use the chicken for making the soup and use the bones you would typically throw away (which have already been roasted) to make the broth.
- Using your slow cooker makes the process even easier. There is no watching a boiling pot. Make it at least a day before you want to use it.
- Cool the broth quickly to prevent bacteria from growing by straining it into a shallow container. The large surface area will allow the broth to cool more quickly than it would in a deep container.
- As the broth cools, the fat will rise to the top and solidify, making it easy to remove and discard. Or keep the fat in the freezer for up to 6 months and use instead of butter to make gravy.
- The collagen from the bones will create a gelatinous broth, which will melt back into a liquid when heated.
- If you don't wish to use all the broth within 24 hours, you can freeze it up to 6 months.

SLOW-COOKER CHICKEN BONE BROTH

Remove meat from 2 deli rotisserie chickens (2 pounds each); reserve meat for chicken soup or another use. In 5- to 6-quart slow cooker, place chicken bones; 6 cups water; 2 tablespoons cider vinegar; ½ teaspoon pepper; 1 large onion, cut into quarters; 2 stalks celery; 2 medium carrots, peeled if desired, cut into 3-inch chunks; 6 cloves garlic; and 4 sprigs each fresh thyme and Italian (flat-leaf) parsley. Cover; cook on Low heat setting 10 to 12 hours. With slotted spoon, remove bones. Pour broth through strainer into shallow container to remove any food particles. Cover; refrigerate overnight. Remove fat layer; discard. Use immediately or refrigerate up to 5 days.

VARIATIONS ▶

Variations

CHEESY CHICKEN AND BROCCOLI SOUP

Prepare as directed—except omit celery and carrots. Add 2 cups broccoli florets with the noodles. Continue as directed. To serve, top each serving of soup with 1 tablespoon shredded Cheddar cheese.

CHICKEN RICE SOUP

Prepare as directed—except substitute 1 cup uncooked regular long-grain white rice for the egg noodles. Cover and cook 15 minutes or until rice and vegetables are tender.

CHICKEN, SPINACH AND TORTELLINI SOUP

Prepare as directed—except omit celery. Substitute 1½ cups frozen cheese-filled tortellini for the egg noodles. After adding remaining ingredients except tortellini, increase cook time to 10 minutes. Add tortellini; cook 3 to 5 minutes longer or until tortellini is tender. Stir in 3 cups fresh spinach and ¼ teaspoon ground nutmeg. Cover and cook 1 to 2 minutes or until spinach is wilted and hot.

ROOT VEGETABLE CHICKEN-PASTA SOUP

Prepare as directed—except add 3 medium peeled and sliced parsnips (1 cup) with the carrots. Add 2 tablespoons chopped fresh or 2 teaspoons dried dill weed with the salt. Substitute 1 cup uncooked orzo or rosamarina pasta (6 ounces) for the egg noodles.

SPICY CHICKEN NOODLE SOUP

Prepare as directed—except add 1 to 2 seeded chopped fresh jalapeño chiles with the celery.

#13

Individual CHICKEN POT PIES

6 SERVINGS   PREP TIME: **40 MINUTES**   START TO FINISH: **1 HOUR 40 MINUTES**

⅓   **cup butter**

⅓   **cup all-purpose flour**

⅓   **cup chopped onion**

½   **teaspoon salt**

¼   **teaspoon pepper**

1¾   **cups chicken broth**

⅔   **cup milk**

3   **cups cut-up cooked chicken or turkey**

2   **cups frozen peas and carrots**

Two-Crust Pastry (page 256)

1. Lightly spray 6 (10-oz) ramekins or custard cups with cooking spray.

2. In 2-quart saucepan, melt butter over medium heat. Stir in flour, onion, salt and pepper. Cook and stir until mixture is bubbly, 2 to 3 minutes. Stir in broth and milk. Heat to boiling, stirring constantly, 3 to 5 minutes, until thickened. Boil and stir 1 minute. Stir in chicken and peas and carrots; remove from heat.

3. Heat oven to 425°F. Prepare pastry as directed in steps 1 and 2 of Two-Crust Pastry. Using floured rolling pin, roll one round of pastry on lightly floured surface into 16-inch round. Using a ramekin or custard cup as a guide, cut dough with sharp knife into 3 circles at least 1 inch larger than ramekin (about 5½ inches in diameter), rerolling pastry if necessary. Repeat with remaining pastry to make 6 pastry circles total. Place ramekins on 15x10x1-inch baking pan. Evenly divide chicken mixture among ramekins. Top each ramekin with pastry round, gently pressing down side of ramekin. Cut a slit in top of each round.

4. Bake 30 to 35 minutes or until golden brown.

1 SERVING: CALORIES 670; TOTAL FAT 43G (SATURATED FAT 14G, TRANS FAT 5G); CHOLESTEROL 80MG; SODIUM 1050MG; TOTAL CARBOHYDRATE 44G (DIETARY FIBER 3G); PROTEIN 25G **EXCHANGES:** 3 STARCH, 2½ LEAN MEAT, 6½ FAT **CARBOHYDRATE CHOICES:** 3

FAMILY-SIZE POT PIE

Prepare as directed—except roll ⅔ of pastry into 13-inch square. Ease into ungreased 9-inch square (2-quart) glass baking dish. Pour chicken mixture into pastry-lined dish. Roll remaining pastry into 11-inch square. Cut out designs with 1-inch cookie cutter. Place square over chicken mixture. Arrange cutouts on pastry. Turn edges of pastry under and flute. Bake about 35 minutes or until golden brown.

Techniques

MAKING POT PIES

For tips on how to make a great gravy, see page 66.

- Pot pies are a great way to use up leftover refrigerated cooked meat, poultry, fish and veggies. Cut into bite-size pieces. Stir any combination of 4 to 5 cups of ingredients into the sauce.
- Larger bite-size pieces of fresh or frozen veggies can be used in place of the peas and carrots, but you'll want to partially cook and drain them before adding to the sauce so they'll be crisp-tender when the pot pie is baked. Try using 1½ cups green beans, bell peppers, broccoli or cauliflower or any combination of these.
- Busy night? Feel free to use refrigerated pie crusts instead of making your own.
- For tips on making pie pastry for your pot pie, see page 257.
- For decorative ways to flute your pot pie crust, see page 258.
- Make extra individual pot pies for an easy dinner later in the week. Let cool at room temperature for 30 minutes after baking. Cover loosely and refrigerate up to 3 days. When ready to bake, uncover and place on cookie sheet. Bake at 375°F for 20 to 30 minutes or until a table knife inserted in center feels hot when touched with a finger.

VARIATIONS ▶

Variations

CHICKEN DIVAN POT PIES
Prepare as directed—except substitute 1 box (9 ounces) partially cooked frozen broccoli cuts for the peas and carrots. Stir 1 teaspoon curry powder and a few drops red pepper sauce into flour mixture before cooking. Continue as directed.

COLORFUL VEGGIE POT PIES
Prepare as directed—except substitute 1 cup chopped bell pepper (any color) for 1 cup of the peas and carrots. Add ½ teaspoon dried thyme leaves with the vegetables.

NEW ORLEANS POT PIES
Prepare as directed—except add 1½ teaspoons Cajun seasoning with salt and pepper. Decrease chicken to 2 cups. Omit peas and carrots. Add 2 cups frozen sliced okra and 1 cup frozen cooked deveined peeled tiny (150–200) shrimp.

ONE-DISH POT PIES
Prepare as directed—except roll two-thirds of pastry into 13-inch square. Ease into ungreased 9-inch square (2-quart) glass baking dish. Pour chicken mixture into pastry-lined dish. Roll remaining pastry into 11-inch square. Cut out designs with 1-inch cookie cutter. Place square over chicken mixture. Arrange cutouts on pastry. Turn edges of pastry under and flute. Bake about 35 minutes or until golden brown.

PORTABELLA CHICKEN POT PIES
Prepare as directed—except add 1½ cups sliced fresh baby portabella mushrooms to the flour mixture before cooking in step 2. Continue as directed.

TUNA POT PIES
Prepare as directed—except substitute 1 can (12 ounces) tuna in water, drained, for the chicken.

14

Spiced-Up
CALIFORNIA BURGERS

4 BURGERS   PREP TIME: **25 MINUTES**   START TO FINISH: **25 MINUTES**

1   **lb lean (at least 80%) ground beef**

5   **medium green onions, sliced (⅓ cup)**

½   **teaspoon salt**

¼   **teaspoon pepper**

¼   **cup barbecue sauce**

4   **slices pepper Jack cheese**

4   **burger buns, split**

4   **leaves romaine lettuce**

4   **slices tomato**

½   **cup French-fried onions (from 2.8-oz can)**

1. Heat coals or gas grill according to manufacturer's directions for medium-high direct heat. In large bowl, mix beef, green onions, salt and pepper. Shape mixture into 4 patties, about ½ inch thick.

2. Place patties on grill over medium-high heat. Cover grill; cook 8 to 12 minutes, turning once, until meat thermometer inserted in center of patties reads 160°F. Top each burger with 1 tablespoon barbecue sauce and 1 slice cheese. Cover grill; cook about 30 seconds longer or until cheese begins to melt.

3. Remove burgers from grill; cover to keep warm. Place buns, cut sides down, on grill. Cover grill; cook about 1 minute or until golden brown.

4. On bun bottoms, layer lettuce and tomato. Top with burgers and French-fried onions; cover with bun tops.

1 BURGER: CALORIES 490; TOTAL FAT 25G (SATURATED FAT 11G, TRANS FAT 2G); CHOLESTEROL 95MG; SODIUM 990MG; TOTAL CARBOHYDRATE 35G (DIETARY FIBER 2G); PROTEIN 31G **EXCHANGES:** 1½ STARCH, ½ OTHER CARBOHYDRATE, ½ VEGETABLE, 3½ MEDIUM-FAT MEAT, 1½ FAT **CARBOHYDRATE CHOICES:** 2

MAKING THE BEST BURGERS

- Loosely pack the burger ingredients into 4 balls; press into patties. Press any cracks together. (A loosely packed burger will be more tender than a tightly packed one.)
- Place cold burgers on the grill. (Do not let meat come to room temperature for better grilling success.)
- Flip burgers only once to prevent them from falling apart while grilling.
- Don't press burgers. This causes the fat to release from the burgers (making them dry) while feeding the flames of the grill (which can burn the burgers).
- Toasting the buns helps keep them from getting soggy from the moist burger ingredients.

GRILLING TIPS

- Heat grill to temperature specified in the recipe. (If using charcoal, heat coals until they are glowing red, mostly covered with ash, and you can hold the palm of your hand near the rack while timing how long you can comfortably keep it there:

    2 seconds = high heat

    3 seconds = medium-high heat

    4 seconds = medium heat

    5 seconds = low heat

- Grill burgers directly over the heat.
- If flare-ups happen, move burgers to a different part of the grill, move briquettes farther apart (for charcoal) or turn burners off until flames extinguish (for gas).

VARIATIONS ▶

Variations

BACON-CHEDDAR BURGERS

Prepare as directed—except substitute chopped onion for the green onions and Cheddar cheese for the pepper Jack cheese. Omit lettuce and tomato, if desired. Top burgers with 1 or 2 slices crisply cooked bacon before topping with bun tops.

BLACK-AND-BLUE BURGERS

Prepare as directed—except substitute ¼ cup finely chopped onion for the green onion, increase pepper to 1¼ teaspoons, omit barbecue sauce and substitute ⅓ cup crumbled blue cheese for the pepper Jack cheese. Omit tomato and French-fried onions.

MUSHROOM-SWISS BURGERS

Prepare as directed—except omit barbecue sauce, substitute Swiss cheese for the pepper Jack cheese and omit lettuce and tomato and French-fried onions. While burgers are cooking, in 8-inch skillet, cook 2 teaspoons butter and 1 cup sliced mushrooms over medium heat, stirring, 2 to 3 minutes or until tender. Top burgers with mushrooms before adding bun tops.

BUN OPTIONS

Serve these burgers on other types of buns instead of traditional burger buns. Try onion or pretzel buns, Kaiser rolls, Brioche buns or bagels.

SAUCY SUBSTITUTION

Choose your favorite sauce (or what you have on hand) for these burgers instead of using barbecue sauce. Try steak sauce, salsa, pesto, blue cheese or Thousand Island dressing.

#15

Easy
BEEF TACOS

8 TACOS   PREP TIME: **15 MINUTES**   START TO FINISH: **30 MINUTES**

BEEF TACO MEAT

- **1   lb lean (at least 80%) ground beef**
- **1   medium onion, chopped (½ cup)**
- **2   cloves garlic, finely chopped**
- **1   medium jalapeño chile, seeded, finely chopped (2 tablespoons)**
- **½   cup salsa**
- **1   tablespoon chili powder**
- **1   teaspoon ground cumin**
- **1   teaspoon dried oregano leaves**
- **½   teaspoon salt**
- **¼   teaspoon pepper**

TACO TOPPINGS AND TORTILLAS

- **8   (6-inch) flour tortillas or stand-and-stuff hard taco shells**

   Shredded lettuce, shredded cheese, chopped tomato and sour cream, if desired

1. In 10-inch nonstick skillet, cook beef, onion, garlic and jalapeño over medium-high heat 8 to 10 minutes, stirring occasionally, until thoroughly cooked; drain. Stir in remaining ingredients. Cook 1 to 2 minutes longer or until hot.

2. Spoon beef onto tortillas; top with toppings. Serve immediately.

1 TACO: CALORIES 200; TOTAL FAT 9G (SATURATED FAT 3.5G, TRANS FAT 0G); CHOLESTEROL 35MG; SODIUM 520MG; TOTAL CARBOHYDRATE 17G (DIETARY FIBER 2G); PROTEIN 12G **EXCHANGES:** 1 STARCH, 1 MEDIUM-FAT MEAT, ½FAT **CARBOHYDRATE CHOICES:** 1

TEST KITCHEN TIP

Make a double batch of the Beef Taco meat to have on hand for quick meals. Freeze it in small containers to pull out when there's no time for cooking.

MAKING GREAT TACOS

- Starting with well-seasoned taco meat is the biggest secret to delicious tacos.
- Cooking the beef with onion, garlic and jalapeño not only saves prep time but it also allows the flavors to blend into the meat.
- Ground turkey, chicken or pork could be substituted for the ground beef.
- Cooking the beef mixture with the seasonings for a few minutes not only heats the seasonings but also helps the flavors to blend.

ADDING TOPPINGS

Toppings make it easy to customize tacos and also add interest through color, texture and flavor.

- Offer a variety of toppings so people can personalize the tacos to their liking.
- Consider toppings that add color and crunch, sauciness for moisture and creaminess to complement the heat from the meat.

VARIATIONS ▶

Variations

BLACK BEAN AND RICE TACOS
Prepare as directed—except omit ground beef. Heat 1 tablespoon vegetable oil in skillet over medium-high heat. Cook onion, garlic and jalapeño in oil 5 to 6 minutes or until tender. Stir in 1 cup cooked white or brown rice, 1 can (15 ounces) rinsed and drained black beans and ¼ cup water with the seasonings. Increase salsa to 1 cup. Cook 5 to 8 minutes or until heated through.

CHICKEN TACOS
Prepare as directed—except heat 1 tablespoon vegetable oil in 10-inch nonstick skillet and substitute 1 pound boneless skinless chicken breast, cut into ¼-inch strips, for the ground beef.

HEARTY BURRITOS
Prepare as directed—except omit taco toppings. Spread ¼ cup heated refried beans and ¼ cup cooked Spanish rice on each of 4 flour tortillas (9 or 10 inch). Divide beef or chicken mixture among tortillas. Sprinkle each burrito with 2 tablespoons shredded Cheddar cheese, 1 tablespoon chopped tomato and 1 tablespoon sour cream. Fold bottom of each tortilla 1 inch over filling. Fold sides in, overlapping to enclose filling. Fold top over sides.

SMOKY ADOBO BEEF TACOS
Prepare as directed—except substitute 1 or 2 chopped chiles in adobo sauce for the jalalpeño. Substitute ground ancho chile pepper for the chili powder and add 1 teaspoon smoked paprika with the ground ancho chile. Stir 2 tablespoons chopped fresh cilantro into the cooked beef mixture before spooning onto tortillas.

SPICY BEEF TACOS
Prepare as directed—except substitute 1 habanero chile for the jalapeño.

Savory
MEAT LOAF

6 SERVINGS   PREP TIME: **20 MINUTES**   START TO FINISH: **1 HOUR 40 MINUTES**

1½   **lb lean ground beef**

1   **cup milk**

1   **tablespoon Worcestershire sauce**

1   **teaspoon chopped fresh sage leaves or ¼ teaspoon dried sage leaves**

½   **teaspoon salt**

½   **teaspoon ground mustard**

¼   **teaspoon pepper**

1   **clove garlic, finely chopped, or ⅛ teaspoon garlic powder**

1   **egg**

3   **slices bread, torn into small pieces**

1   **small onion, chopped (⅓ cup)**

½   **cup ketchup, chili sauce or barbecue sauce**

1. Heat oven to 350°F. In large bowl, mix all ingredients except ketchup. Spread mixture in ungreased 8x4- or 9x5-inch loaf pan, or shape into 9x5-inch loaf in 13x9-inch pan. Spread ketchup over top.

2. Insert ovenproof meat thermometer so tip is in center of loaf. Bake uncovered 1 hour to 1 hour 15 minutes or until beef is no longer pink in center and thermometer reads 160°F; drain fat. Let stand 5 minutes; remove from pan.

1 SERVING: CALORIES 290; TOTAL FAT 15G (SATURATED FAT 6G, TRANS FAT 0.5G); CHOLESTEROL 105MG; SODIUM 540MG; TOTAL CARBOHYDRATE 16G (DIETARY FIBER 0G); PROTEIN 23G **EXCHANGES:** ½ STARCH, ½ OTHER CARBOHYDRATE, 3 LEAN MEAT, 1 FAT **CARBOHYDRATE CHOICES:** 1

TEST KITCHEN TIP

Use lean ground beef (at least 80% lean) so the meat loaf isn't swimming in fat while cooking. You'll get a nice brown color and pleasing texture (not greasy) when you devour it.

MAKING A GREAT MEAT LOAF

- Egg and bread crumbs in the correct proportions to the meat are the secret to meat loaves that hold their shape when cutting.
- One-half cup dry bread crumbs or ¾ cup quick-cooking oats can be substituted for the 3 slices bread. Use whatever you have on hand. (It's a great place to use up the ends of a loaf of bread.)
- When shaping the meat mixture into a loaf, be sure to smooth out any cracks before cooking.
- Spreading the top of the meat loaf with ketchup (or other sauce) will add appeal to the meat loaf's appearance and add flavor.
- Insert an ovenproof meat thermometer so the tip is in the center of loaf, and cook until the thermometer reads 160°F.
- Drain fat from the meat loaf after cooking so the meat loaf won't be wet from the fat and will hold its shape when cut.
- Let the meat loaf stand 5 minutes for the temperature to reach 165°F and allow it to set up for easier slicing.
- Remove slices from the pan with a pancake turner to help hold their shape.

VARIATIONS ▶

Variations

BASIL MEAT LOAF
Prepare as directed—except substitute 2 tablespoons chopped fresh basil leaves for the sage leaves.

CHEESY MEAT LOAF
Prepare as directed—except while meat loaf is cooking, cut 3 slices (1 ounce each) Cheddar, Colby-Monterey Jack or Swiss cheese diagonally in half. During last few minutes of cooking, arrange slices on top of meat loaf. Cook until thermometer reaches 160°F and cheese is melted.

ITALIAN MEAT LOAF
Prepare as directed—except substitute Italian seasoning for the sage and spaghetti sauce for the ketchup.

MEAT LOAF AND MASHED POTATOES DINNER
Prepare as directed. Place slices of meat loaf onto dinner plates. Top each with about ½ cup hot mashed potatoes or sweet potatoes, 3 stalks cooked broccoli and 2 tablespoons gravy.

MEAT LOAF SANDWICH
Prepare as directed. Spread one side of each of 2 slices bread with about 1 tablespoon ketchup, chili sauce or barbecue sauce. Top each slice with 1 slice meat loaf. Add lettuce and tomato slices, if desired. Top with remaining slice of bread, sauce side down.

Perfectly
GRILLED STEAKS

4 SERVINGS   PREP TIME: **10 MINUTES**   START TO FINISH: **55 MINUTES**

6 **cloves garlic, finely chopped**

¼ **cup balsamic vinegar**

1 **tablespoon honey**

2 **teaspoons Worcestershire sauce**

1 **teaspoon salt**

½ **teaspoon cracked pepper**

2 **beef rib eye steaks, about 1 inch thick (8 to 10 oz each)**

   Vegetable oil

2 **tablespoons finely chopped green onions (2 medium)**

½ **cup crumbled blue cheese (2 oz), if desired**

1. In small bowl, stir garlic, balsamic vinegar, honey, Worcestershire sauce, salt and pepper with whisk until well blended. Place steaks in 1-gallon resealable food-storage plastic bag. Pour marinade over steaks; seal. Shake bag to coat steaks. Marinate at room temperature 30 minutes.

2. Meanwhile, heat coals or gas grill according to manufacturer's directions for medium direct heat. Remove steaks from marinade.

3. Brush grill with vegetable oil. Place steaks on grill over medium heat. Cover grill; cook 10 to 15 minutes for medium doneness (160°F), turning once. Remove steaks to heatproof platter; let stand 5 minutes. Sprinkle with green onions and blue cheese.

1 SERVING: CALORIES 220; TOTAL FAT 8G (SATURATED FAT 3G, TRANS FAT 0G); CHOLESTEROL 80MG; SODIUM 660MG; TOTAL CARBOHYDRATE 10G (DIETARY FIBER 0G); PROTEIN 28G **EXCHANGES:** ½ OTHER CARBOHYDRATE, 2 VERY LEAN MEAT, 2 LEAN MEAT **CARBOHYDRATE CHOICES:** ½

Techniques

GETTING THE STEAKS READY

Start by seasoning the steaks and letting them marinate at room temperature. Thirty minutes is all it takes for flavor and food safety. This allows the steaks to warm up so they'll cook properly (cold steaks contract and can become tough) and allows the seasoning to start flavoring them. The salt will help the steaks retain moisture during cooking.

GETTING THE GRILL READY

Heat the grill before cooking the steaks. Make sure the grill has had enough time to get up to temperature before the meat is added.

• Grilling steaks at medium heat enables you to get a perfectly done steak inside without burning it on the outside.

• To check if your grill is to temperature, hold the palm of your hand near the grill rack. If you can hold it there comfortably for 4 seconds, it's medium heat. If you can't hold it that long, it's too hot. If you can hold it longer, it's too cool.

CONTROLLING THE HEAT

It takes some effort to maintain even heat, even with a gas grill. The wind, air temperature and how often you lift the lid can change the temperature. Try to maintain the heat at medium for steaks that are perfectly done. Follow the manufacturer's directions for maintaining the heat and use these general guidelines:

GAS/ELECTRIC GRILL: If the heat is too high, use a lower heat setting. If the heat is too low, use a higher heat setting.

CHARCOAL GRILL: If the coals are too hot, spread them out or close the vents halfway. If they're too cool, either move the coals closer together, knock the ashes off by tapping them with long-handled tongs or open the air vents.

PREVENTING FLARE-UPS

Fats and sugary sauces dripping through the grill racks can cause flare-ups that burn the food and cause a fire hazard. Prevent flare-ups by:

- Trimming excess fat from steaks
- Keeping the bottom of the grill uncovered so the grease can drain easily into the grease catch pan
- Keeping the grill bottom and catch pan clean and debris free
- Adding sugary sauces only during the last 10 to 15 minutes of cooking to prevent them from burning

TAMING FLARE-UPS

- For gas grills, move the steaks to a different area of the grill rack. Cover the grill to extinguish the flames.
- For a charcoal grill, spread the coals farther apart or move the food and spritz the flames with water from a spray bottle. When the flames are extinguished, move the steaks back to the desired area.
- For a gas or electric grill, turn all burners off. NEVER USE WATER TO EXTINGUISH FLAMES ON A GAS OR ELECTRIC GRILL. When the flames are extinguished, re-light the grill.

OILING THE GRILL GRATE

Always oil the grill grate before cooking to prevent sticking. Use a neutral-flavored oil, such as vegetable oil. Do not use olive oil. Moisten a paper towel or grill brush with a little oil, and use long-handled tongs to brush it on the grate.

COOKING THE STEAKS

Grill the steaks on one side until they easily lift from the grill grate. Turn the steaks only once to keep them from drying out.

TECHNIQUES ▶
AND VARIATIONS

PERFECTLY GRILLED STEAKS (CONTINUED)

MAKING SEAR MARKS

Everyone loves the look and flavor of steaks with grill marks.

- Place steaks on hot grill. Cover; grill steaks about 2 minutes without moving them or until dark sear marks are visible on the bottom; turn steaks over. Continue grilling until desired doneness.
- To make crosshatch grill marks, do not turn steaks. Rotate them at a 45° angle. Grill 2 minutes longer or until dark sear marks are visible on the bottom; turn steaks over. Continue grilling until desired doneness.

DETERMINING DONENESS

Grilling time is based on medium doneness or 160°F. For medium-rare, cook steaks to 145°F, and for well-done, cook steaks to 170°F.

- Use a meat thermometer inserted into the thickest part of the steak (not touching a bone) to measure the temperature.
- Let the steak rest 5 minutes before serving to allow the juices to spread throughout the steak and soften the fibers.

Variations

BLACK-AND-BLUE STEAKS: Prepare as directed—except after removing steaks from marinade, sprinkle both sides of steaks with an additional 1½ teaspoons cracked pepper; press lightly into steak. To serve, top steaks with the green onions and blue cheese.

GARLICKY GRILLED STEAKS: Prepare as directed—except add 2 or 3 finely chopped cloves garlic with the balsamic vinegar.

STEAK SALAD WITH BALSAMIC DRESSING: Prepare as directed—except place 5 ounces (5 cups) baby arugula on serving platter. Arrange halved cherry tomatoes, sliced avocado, sliced red onion and thinly sliced steak over arugula. Drizzle with Creamy Balsamic Dressing (page 174).

STEAKS WITH CARAMELIZED ONIONS: Prepare Caramelized Onions (page 46); keep warm. Prepare steaks as directed—except omit green onions. Serve steaks with caramelized onions.

STEAKS WITH STEAK SAUCE: Prepare as directed—except after removing steaks from marinade, do not discard marinade. In 8-inch nonstick pan, melt 2 tablespoons butter over medium heat. Stir in reserved marinade and 1 tablespoon Dijon mustard with whisk and cook 3 to 4 minutes, stirring frequently, until slightly thickened. Serve with steak.

BEEF STEW

8 SERVINGS   PREP TIME: **15 MINUTES**   START TO FINISH: **3 HOURS 45 MINUTES**

1   lb beef stew meat, cut into ½-inch pieces

1   medium onion, cut into 8 wedges

1   bag (8 oz) ready-to-eat baby-cut carrots (about 30)

1   can (14.5 oz) diced tomatoes, undrained

1   can (10½ oz) condensed beef broth

1   can (8 oz) tomato sauce

⅓   cup all-purpose flour

1   tablespoon Worcestershire sauce

1   teaspoon salt

1   teaspoon sugar

1   teaspoon dried marjoram leaves

¼   teaspoon pepper

12   small red potatoes (1½ lb), cut into quarters

2   cups sliced fresh mushrooms (about 5 oz) or 1 package (about 3.5 oz) fresh shiitake mushrooms, sliced

1. Heat oven to 325°F. In 4-quart ovenproof Dutch oven, mix all ingredients except potatoes and mushrooms. Cover and bake 2 hours, stirring once.

2. Stir in potatoes and mushrooms. Cover and bake 1 hour to 1 hour 30 minutes longer or until beef and vegetables are tender.

1 SERVING: CALORIES 230; TOTAL FAT 6G (SATURATED FAT 2.5G, TRANS FAT 0G); CHOLESTEROL 30MG; SODIUM 830MG; TOTAL CARBOHYDRATE 28G (DIETARY FIBER 4G); PROTEIN 15G **EXCHANGES:** 1 STARCH, ½ OTHER CARBOHYDRATE, 1½ VEGETABLE, 1 LEAN MEAT,½FAT **CARBOHYDRATE CHOICES:** 2

BEST-EVER BEEF STEW

Look for beef stew meat already trimmed and cut into ½- to 1-inch pieces in the meat department.

- Be sure all pieces of meat are ½ inch so that they will all be done at the same time. Trim to uniform size if necessary.
- Cooking stew for a long period of time on low heat ensures that the meat will be tender. Less-expensive cuts of meat, such as stew meat, become tough if cooked at high temperatures.
- Test several pieces of meat and veggies with a fork to be sure they are all tender before serving. If some aren't quite cooked long enough, continue cooking until all are tender.

VARIATIONS ▶

Variations

BEEF STEW DINNER
Prepare as directed. Spoon hot cooked rice, pasta or mashed potatoes into soup bowls; top with stew.

CHUNKY TOMATO-PEPPER BEEF STEW
Prepare as directed—except add 1 cup diced bell pepper (any color) with the onion; omit mushrooms. Omit tomato sauce and add 1 additional can (14.5 ounces) diced tomatoes, undrained.

CONFETTI BEEF STEW
Prepare as directed—except omit potatoes. Bake 2 hours. Add 1 cup frozen cut green beans and 1 cup frozen corn in step 2.

HARVEST BEEF STEW
Prepare as directed—except decrease potatoes to 6. Omit mushrooms. Add 1 package (9 ounces) frozen whole kernel corn and 2 cups sliced zucchini with the potatoes.

SLOW-COOKER BEEF STEW
Prepare as directed—except instead of cutting onion into wedges, chop onion (about 1½ cups). Omit tomato sauce. Increase flour to 1½ cup. Spray 3½- to 6-quart slow cooker with cooking spray. In slow cooker, mix all ingredients except beef. Add beef (do not stir). Cover; cook on Low heat setting 8 to 9 hours. Stir well before serving.

SWEET POTATO–PEA BEEF STEW
Prepare as directed—except substitute 2 cups cubed peeled sweet potatoes for the potatoes. Omit mushrooms. Stir in 2 cups frozen peas during last 15 minutes of cooking.

Garlic Herb
PORK CHOPS

4 SERVINGS   PREP TIME: **20 MINUTES**   START TO FINISH: **20 MINUTES**

- **4** **boneless thin-cut pork loin chops (about 1 lb)**
- **1** **teaspoon garlic salt**
- **¼** **cup all-purpose flour**
- **¾** **cup panko crispy bread crumbs**
- **1** **tablespoon chopped fresh parsley**
- **2** **teaspoons chopped fresh basil**
- **2** **teaspoons chopped fresh oregano**
- **3** **tablespoons milk**
- **3** **tablespoons olive or vegetable oil**

1. Between pieces of plastic wrap or waxed paper, place each pork chop; gently pound with flat side of meat mallet or rolling pin until about ¼ inch thick. Sprinkle both sides of chops with garlic salt.

2. Place flour in shallow bowl. In another shallow bowl, mix bread crumbs, parsley, basil and oregano. Place milk in third shallow bowl. Dip each pork chop in flour, then dip in milk. Coat well with bread crumb mixture.

3. In 12-inch nonstick skillet, heat oil over medium heat. Cook pork in oil 7 to 9 minutes, turning once, until browned and no longer pink in center.

1 SERVING: CALORIES 350; TOTAL FAT 16G (SATURATED FAT 3G, TRANS FAT 0G); CHOLESTEROL 70MG; SODIUM 350MG; TOTAL CARBOHYDRATE 22G (DIETARY FIBER 0G); PROTEIN 29G **EXCHANGES:** 1½ OTHER CARBOHYDRATE, 4 VERY LEAN MEAT, 3 FAT **CARBOHYDRATE CHOICES:** 1½

INGREDIENT WHYS

THIN PORK CHOPS: Starting with thin chops means it takes less time to pound them. Pounding the pork chops ensures that they cook evenly and quickly and remain tender and moist.

PANKO BREAD CRUMBS: Choosing panko crispy bread crumbs helps ensure a crisp crust on the pork chops.

FRESH HERBS: Herbs add a lot of color and flavor to the pork chops. If fresh herbs are not available, substitute 1 teaspoon dried parsley flakes, ½ teaspoon dried basil leaves and ½ teaspoon dried oregano leaves for the fresh herbs.

THE SECRETS OF DREDGING

- Dredging means lightly coating food with flour and possibly other ingredients to help the food retain moisture during cooking and aid in browning.
- Dredging the pork chops in flour first helps the bread crumb mixture adhere to the chops during cooking.
- If you use one hand for coating the pork chops in flour and dipping in milk and your other hand for coating them in the bread crumb mixture, you can keep the amount of coating ingredients stuck to your fingers to a minimum.

PANFRYING TIPS

- Panfrying uses a small amount of oil in a pan, cooking the food quickly to keep coatings crisp and tender cuts of meat tender.
- A nonstick skillet helps prevent the coating from sticking to the pan.
- Heat the oil in the skillet until hot before adding the meat.
- Cook (without moving the meat around) until the bottom sides are browned before turning to cook the other side.
- Turn the meat only once to prevent it from overcooking and disturbing the coating.

VARIATIONS ▶

Variations

BREADED SOUTHWEST PORK CHOPS
Prepare as directed—except omit basil and oregano. Add 1 tablespoon chili powder to the bread crumbs. Serve chops with corn and tomato salsa.

DIJON-HERB PORK CHOPS
Prepare as directed—except whisk 2 teaspoons Dijon mustard into milk. Continue as directed.

LEMON-CHIVE PORK CHOPS
Prepare as directed—except omit parsley, basil and oregano. Add 1½ tablespoons chopped fresh chives and 1 tablespoon grated lemon zest to the bread crumbs.

ORANGE-GINGER PORK CHOPS
Prepare as directed—except omit basil and oregano. Add 2 teaspoons grated orange zest and ¾ teaspoon ground ginger to the bread crumbs. Combine 3 tablespoons maple syrup, 1 tablespoon soy sauce, 1 tablespoon fresh orange juice and ¼ teaspoon ground ginger; mix well. Serve with the pork chops.

PORK CHOPS PICCATA
Prepare as directed—except remove cooked pork chops to heatproof platter; cover to keep warm. Melt 2 tablespoons butter in skillet over medium heat. Stir in 1½ tablespoons all-purpose flour and ¼ teaspoon each salt and pepper; cook until bubbly. Gradually stir in ¾ cup chicken broth, ⅔ cup white wine and 1 tablespoon fresh lemon juice. Stir constantly until mixture thickens slightly and comes to a boil. Boil and stir 1 minute. Serve sauce over the pork chops.

Slow-Cooker
BBQ PULLED PORK SANDWICHES

12 SANDWICHES   PREP TIME: **20 MINUTES**   START TO FINISH: **10 HOURS 20 MINUTES**

1 **large onion, sliced**

4 **cloves garlic, thinly sliced**

2 **tablespoons packed brown sugar**

1 **tablespoon paprika**

1½ **teaspoons salt**

1½ **teaspoons ground mustard**

1 **teaspoon finely crushed dried chipotle chili**

1 **boneless pork shoulder, trimmed of fat (4 to 5 lb)**

1½ to 2 **cups barbecue sauce**

10 **kaiser rolls or burger buns, split**

1. Spray 4- to 6-quart slow cooker with cooking spray. Place onions and garlic in slow cooker.

2. In small bowl, stir together brown sugar, paprika, salt, mustard and chili pepper. Rub mixture evenly over pork. Place pork in slow cooker.

3. Cover and cook on Low heat setting 8 to 10 hours until very tender and pork shreds easily. Remove pork from slow cooker; cool slightly. Strain cooking liquid; discard liquid that is strained off. Using 2 forks, shred pork, removing fat. Return pork to slow cooker. Stir in enough barbecue sauce to make pork saucy. Increase heat setting to High; cover and cook 45 minutes longer or until hot.

4. Spoon pork into rolls. Serve with additional barbecue sauce, if desired.

1 SANDWICH: CALORIES 500; TOTAL FAT 20G (SATURATED FAT 6G, TRANS FAT 0.5G); CHOLESTEROL 95MG; SODIUM 960MG; TOTAL CARBOHYDRATE 43G (DIETARY FIBER 2G); PROTEIN 36G **EXCHANGES:** 2 STARCH, 1 OTHER CARBOHYDRATE, 4 VERY LEAN MEAT, 3½ FAT **CARBOHYDRATE CHOICES:** 3

TIPS FOR SLOW-COOKER SUCCESS

USING THE SLOW-COOKER

- Use the size slow cooker called for in the recipe. Slow cookers are most efficient when they are two-thirds to three-fourths full. Over- or underfilling your slow cooker could affect the cook time and texture of the cooked food.
- For easy cleanup, spray the inside of the slow cooker insert with cooking spray.
- Always keep your slow cooker covered for the time stated in the recipe. Each time you remove the cover, it allows the heat to escape, adding 15 to 20 minutes to the cook time.
- Only remove the cover if a recipe specifies and only after the first 2 hours of cooking.

PREPPING INGREDIENTS

- Cut most ingredients into uniform sizes for the best cooking results.
- Root vegetables take longer to cook than other vegetables, so cut them into smaller pieces and place at the bottom of the slow cooker.
- The onions are used in this recipe to lift the meat away from the bottom of the slow cooker so that the fat can melt into them during cooking. For the best flavor and texture of the pork, we recommend discarding the cooked onions with the cooking liquid as they can be greasy, adding a greasiness to the pork as well as diluting the flavor.
- Make sure raw potatoes are covered with liquid to prevent them from darkening.
- Don't add more liquid or more vegetables (which can add more liquid to the dish as they cook) than specified in a recipe. Liquids don't evaporate from the slow cooker and foods will remain moist.
- Remove poultry skin and excess fat from meats before cooking to reduce fat in the dish.
- Brown meat and poultry in a skillet before adding to the slow cooker to add flavor and color.

VARIATIONS ▶

Variations

COLESLAW-TOPPED PORK SANDWICHES

Prepare as directed. Top pork in rolls with coleslaw before serving.

MAPLE-BOURBON BBQ PULLED PORK SANDWICHES

Prepare as directed—except stir 2 tablespoons each real maple syrup and bourbon into barbecue sauce before stirring into pork.

MEXICAN GARLIC-LIME SHREDDED PORK SANDWICHES

Prepare as directed—except omit rub ingredients called for in step 2 and instead rub pork with a mixture of 1 tablespoon chili powder, 2 teaspoons ground cumin, 2 teaspoons dried oregano leaves, 1½ teaspoons salt and 1½ teaspoons finely crushed dried chipotle chile. Reserve ½ cup cooking liquid, discarding onions. After shredding pork, substitute 1 cup fresh orange juice and ¼ cup fresh lime juice for the barbecue sauce. Stir in reserved cooking liquid.

ORANGE-THYME PULLED PORK SANDWICHES

Prepare as directed—except omit brown sugar, paprika, ground mustard and finely crushed dried chipotle chile. Mix 1 teaspoon each grated orange zest and dried thyme leaves and 2 chopped green onions with the salt and pepper. Brush pork with 1 to 2 tablespoons balsamic vinegar before rubbing with orange mixture.

SHREDDED PORK TACO PIZZA

In the Legendary Chicken Taco Pizza (page 60), substitute either Mexican Garlic-Lime Shredded Pork or BBQ Pulled Pork for the chicken.

Slow-Cooker
BARBECUED RIBS

4 SERVINGS   PREP TIME: **15 MINUTES**   START TO FINISH: **9 HOURS 15 MINUTES**

3½   **lb pork loin back ribs**

¼   **cup packed brown sugar**

3   **tablespoons liquid smoke**

1   **teaspoon salt**

½   **teaspoon pepper**

2   **cloves garlic, chopped**

1   **medium onion, sliced**

½   **cup cola**

1½   **cups barbecue sauce**

1. Spray inside of 4- to 5-quart slow cooker with cooking spray.

2. Remove inner skin from ribs. In small bowl, mix brown sugar, liquid smoke, salt, pepper and garlic; rub mixture into ribs. Cut ribs into 4-inch pieces. Layer ribs and onion in slow cooker. Pour cola over ribs.

3. Cover and cook on Low heat setting 8 to 9 hours or until tender. Remove ribs from slow cooker. Drain and discard liquid.

4. Pour barbecue sauce into shallow bowl. Dip ribs into sauce. Place ribs in slow cooker. Pour any remaining sauce over ribs. Cover and cook on Low heat setting 1 hour.

1 SERVING: CALORIES 750; TOTAL FAT 36G (SATURATED FAT 13G, TRANS FAT 0G); CHOLESTEROL 160MG; SODIUM 1210MG; TOTAL CARBOHYDRATE 63G (DIETARY FIBER 1G); PROTEIN 44G **EXCHANGES:** 4 OTHER CARBOHYDRATE, 6 MEDIUM-FAT MEAT, 1 FAT **CARBOHYDRATE CHOICES:** 4

MAKING TENDER, FALL-OFF-THE-BONE RIBS

Have the butcher cut off the silverskin from the ribs, if possible.

To remove the silverskin yourself, slide a table knife under the membrane and over a bone. Use the knife to loosen and lift the membrane until one end tears free.

Grab the loose end with a paper towel and pull it off. Repeat steps if the membrane won't come off in one piece.

- Spray the slow cooker with cooking spray before adding ingredients to make cleanup a breeze later.
- Cook ribs until they are tender when the meat is pierced with a fork.
- Cooking the ribs with the sauce for an additional hour allows them to soak up the sauce flavor and become so tender they fall off the bone.

SLOW-COOKER TIPS

- Slow cookers should be filled between one-half and two-thirds full. If filled any more or less, the cooking time will be affected and the food may be over- or undercooked.
- Don't be tempted to peek! Every time you lift the lid of a slow cooker, you add at least 20 minutes' cooking time and rob the slow cooker of moisture it's creating to produce moist, tender food.
- This recipe was tested in slow cookers with heating elements in the side and bottom of the cooker, not in cookers that stand only on a heated base. For slow cookers with just a heated base, follow the manufacturer's directions for layering ingredients and choosing a temperature.

VARIATIONS ▶

Variations

BEER-BRAISED BBQ RIBS
Prepare as directed—except substitute mild-flavored beer (such as IPA or American Pale Lager or fruit beer) for the cola.

CHILI-ORANGE RIBS
Prepare as directed—except substitute fresh orange juice for the cola. Omit barbecue sauce. In small saucepan, heat 1 cup chili sauce, ¼ cup orange marmalade, 2 tablespoons Worcestershire sauce and 1 teaspoon ground mustard over medium-low heat, stirring occasionally, until marmalade is melted. Stir in 2 tablespoons chopped fresh chives. Substitute for the barbecue sauce.

HOT-SWEET RIBS
Prepare as directed—except omit barbecue sauce. In small saucepan, heat ½ cup red currant jelly, ⅓ cup hoisin sauce and ¼ teaspoon hot pepper sauce over medium heat, stirring frequently, until jelly is melted. Substitute for the barbecue sauce.

MOLASSES-MUSTARD RIBS
Prepare as directed—except omit barbecue sauce. Mix ½ cup molasses, ⅓ cup Dijon mustard and ⅓ cup cider vinegar or white vinegar. Substitute for the barbecue sauce.

RIBS WITH CHERRY COLA BBQ SAUCE
Prepare as directed—except omit rub mixture on ribs. Substitute ½ teaspoon seasoned salt, ½ teaspoon garlic-pepper blend and ¼ teaspoon ground ginger for the rub. Substitute ½ (12-ounce) can cherry cola for the cola. While ribs are cooking, decrease barbecue sauce to 1 cup; pour into small saucepan. Add remaining cola from cherry cola can, 3 tablespoons cherry preserves and ¼ teaspoon ground ginger. Heat to boiling. Reduce heat to medium-low. Simmer uncovered 15 to 20 minutes, stirring occasionally, until sauce is slightly thickened.

PANFRIED FISH

6 SERVINGS   PREP TIME: **20 MINUTES**   START TO FINISH: **20 MINUTES**

1½ lb perch, red snapper or other medium-firm fish fillets (½ to ¾ inch thick), skin removed

¾ teaspoon salt

¼ teaspoon pepper

1 egg

1 tablespoon water

⅔ cup all-purpose flour, cornmeal or dry bread crumbs

Vegetable oil or shortening

1. Cut fish into 6 serving pieces. Sprinkle both sides with salt and pepper. In small bowl, beat egg and water with fork or whisk until blended. Place flour in shallow dish. Dip fish into egg, then coat with flour.

2. In 12-inch skillet, heat about ⅛ inch oil over medium heat. Fry fish in oil 6 to 8 minutes, turning once, until fish flakes easily with fork and is brown on both sides. (Fish cooks very quickly, especially the thinner tail sections; be careful not to overcook.) Remove with slotted spatula; drain on paper towels.

1 SERVING: CALORIES 200; TOTAL FAT 7G (SATURATED FAT 1.5G, TRANS FAT 0G); CHOLESTEROL 95MG; SODIUM 230MG; TOTAL CARBOHYDRATE 11G (DIETARY FIBER 0G); PROTEIN 24G **EXCHANGES:** 1 STARCH, 3 VERY LEAN MEAT, ½ FAT **CARBOHYDRATE CHOICES:** 1

Techniques

BUYING FISH

- Other types of fish that work well for panfrying are catfish, char, lake perch and rockfish/ocean perch.
- The fish's flesh should be shiny, firm and spring back when touched. Avoid fish with dark edges or brown or yellow discoloration.
- Fish should smell fresh and mild, not fishy or like ammonia.
- Buy and use fish by the sell-buy date.

STORING FISH

- Keep fresh or thawed fish in the original packaging in the coldest part of your refrigerator. Use within 2 days.
- Fish that is packaged in clear plastic wrap on a tray can be frozen as is. For other packaging, fish should be removed and tightly wrapped in freezer plastic bags or foil. Freeze up to 6 months. Thaw overnight in the refrigerator.

COOKING FISH

Fish is naturally delicate and tender, so overcooking makes it dry. Follow the "10-minute rule," cooking fish 10 minutes per inch of thickness.

Cook just until the fish flakes easily with a fork. Insert the tines of the fork gently into the thickest part of the fish and twist slightly. The flesh should begin to separate along the natural lines.

Dip fillets into beaten egg.

Dip fillets in flour on both sides.

Fry fish in ⅛ inch oil, turning once.

Cook until fish flakes easily with fork.

Variations

BROWNED-BUTTER PANFRIED FISH: Prepare as directed—except omit oil. In skillet, heat ¼ cup butter over medium heat 3 to 4 minutes, stirring constantly, until light brown. Coat fish as directed in step 1. Cook in butter as directed in step 2.

CAPRESE PANFRIED FISH: Prepare as directed. Top cooked fish with 1 or 2 thin slices of fresh mozzarella cheese, chopped tomatoes and chopped fresh basil leaves.

GARLIC-BUTTER PANFRIED FISH: Prepare as directed—except omit salt. Substitute crushed garlic-butter-flavored croutons for the flour. (Place croutons in resealable food-storage plastic bag and crush with rolling pin.) Continue as directed.

PANFRIED FISH WITH MANGO SALSA: Prepare as directed—except make Mango Salsa. Before making fish, mix 2 cups diced fresh mango, ¼ cup each chopped fresh cilantro and mint leaves, 2 tablespoons fresh lime juice, 1 tablespoon grated gingerroot and ¼ teaspoon salt. Continue as directed. Serve salsa with fish.

PARMESAN AND LEMON PANFRIED FISH: Prepare as directed—except omit salt and pepper. Substitute ⅓ cup Italian-style panko crispy bread crumbs for the ⅔ cup flour. In shallow dish, mix bread crumbs, ⅓ cup grated Parmesan cheese and 1 teaspoon grated lemon zest. Continue as directed.

Sweet Potato and
CHICK PEA TIKKA MASALA

4 SERVINGS   PREP TIME: **20 MINUTES**   START TO FINISH: **55 MINUTES**

- **2** tablespoons olive oil
- **1** large onion, finely chopped (1 cup)
- **1** tablespoon finely chopped gingerroot
- **1** teaspoon ground cumin
- **1** teaspoon garam masala
- **1** teaspoon ground turmeric
- **1** teaspoon smoked paprika
- **½** teaspoon salt
- **⅛** teaspoon ground red pepper (cayenne)
- **2** cloves garlic, finely chopped
- **1** large sweet potato, peeled, cut into ½-inch cubes (about 2 cups)
- **2** cans (14.5 oz each) fire-roasted diced tomatoes
- **1** can (15 oz) garbanzo beans (chick peas), rinsed, drained
- **1** can (14 oz) unsweetened coconut milk

1. In 12-inch nonstick skillet, heat oil over medium heat. Add onion and cook 2 to 4 minutes or until translucent and tender. Stir in gingerroot, cumin, garam masala, turmeric, paprika, salt, red pepper and garlic, cook 1 minute or until fragrant.

2. Stir in remaining ingredients except coconut milk. Reduce heat to low. Cover; cook 25 to 30 minutes or until sweet potatoes are tender. Stir in coconut milk. Cook uncovered 2 to 3 minutes or until slightly thickened and thoroughly heated.

1 SERVING (1½ CUPS): CALORIES 470; TOTAL FAT 30G (SATURATED FAT 20G, TRANS FAT 0G); CHOLESTEROL 0MG; SODIUM 710MG; TOTAL CARBOHYDRATE 41G (DIETARY FIBER 11G); PROTEIN 9G **EXCHANGES:** ½ STARCH, 2 OTHER CARBOHYDRATE, ½ VEGETABLE, 1 VERY LEAN MEAT, 6 FAT **CARBOHYDRATE CHOICES:** 3

MAKING A CURRY

Start with a flavorful base. Onions, garlic and gingerroot are the basic ingredients that give curry a rich depth of flavor. Sometimes garlic is omitted. The longer these ingredients cook, the richer the flavor and the deeper the color of the curry.

- For some spicy heat, add chopped fresh chiles with the onions. Add one or two chopped seeded jalapeños, depending on your preferred level of spiciness.
- Add lots of spice. Spices are typically the star of the show in curry. The combinations used are often a signature of the cook. Feel free to experiment with different combinations to come up with your own unique flavor or to vary the flavor of the dish.
- Add spices early in the cooking process so that they have plenty of time to develop their flavors and mingle together.
- Toasting the spices before adding other ingredients brings out their flavors, adding a warm, earthy, toasted note that the raw spices can't give.
- Watch spices carefully as they can burn quickly. Use your nose to help you know when they are toasted. (When you smell them, they are done!)

COOKING VEGETABLES AND MEAT

- Add bite-size pieces of vegetables that need to be cooked when you add the spices.
- If adding raw meat, brown it in a separate skillet before adding it to your curry. Choose tender cuts because the cooking time of a curry is fairly short, so there isn't the time necessary to make tough cuts tender. Chicken, pork chops or sirloin are good choices.
- Liquid needs to be present for the vegetables and meat to cook. We've used tomatoes here. Or add bite-size pieces of cooked meat when you add your thickener, just so that they can warm up.

ADDING BODY

- Coconut milk, yogurt, pureed or diced tomatoes or spinach are some of the most common ways to thicken your curry. Adding one of these ingredients brings all the ingredients together into one symphony of a dish.

VARIATIONS ▶

Variations

BUTTERNUT SQUASH TIKKA MASALA
Prepare as directed—except substitute 2 cups ½-inch cubes butternut squash for the sweet potato.

CAULIFLOWER AND CHICK PEA TIKKA MASALA
Prepare as directed—except substitute 2 cups cauliflower florets for the sweet potato. Decrease cook time in step 2 to 16 to 22 minutes or until the cauliflower is tender.

CHICKEN TIKKA MASALA
Prepare as directed—except add 1 cup cut-up rotisserie chicken with the coconut milk.

SHRIMP TIKKA MASALA
Prepare as directed—except add 3 cups peeled deveined uncooked medium shrimp (rinsed with cold water to thaw, if frozen) with the coconut milk. Increase cook time to 5 to 7 minutes or until shrimp are pink and mixture is slightly thickened.

TIKKA MASALA WITH CILANTRO-LIME RICE
Prepare as directed. Serve with Cilantro-Lime Rice (page 150).

#24 ORANGE-SESAME TOFU
with Broccoli

4 SERVINGS   PREP TIME: **35 MINUTES**   START TO FINISH: **55 MINUTES**

2¼ **cups water**

1 **cup uncooked extra long-grain brown rice**

1 **tablespoon coconut oil**

⅛ **teaspoon salt**

3 **tablespoons sweet chili sauce**

3 **tablespoons tamari or soy sauce**

1 **teaspoon toasted or dark sesame oil**

1 **package (12 oz) extra-firm water-packed tofu, drained, cut into 1-inch cubes**

2 **tablespoons vegetable oil**

4 **cups fresh broccoli florets**

1 **large red bell pepper, cut into 2-inch strips**

2 **teaspoons grated orange zest**

⅔ **cup fresh orange juice**

2 **teaspoons cornstarch**

1. In 2-quart saucepan, heat 2 cups water, rice, coconut oil and salt to boiling. Reduce heat to low. Cover; simmer 45 to 50 minutes.

2. Meanwhile, in medium bowl, mix chili sauce, tamari and sesame oil. Stir in tofu; let stand 15 minutes. Drain, reserving sauce.

3. In 12-inch nonstick skillet, heat 1 tablespoon vegetable oil over medium heat. Cook tofu in oil about 5 minutes, stirring frequently, until lightly browned on all sides. Remove from skillet; set aside.

4. In same skillet, heat remaining 1 tablespoon vegetable oil over medium heat. Cook broccoli and bell pepper in oil 3 minutes, stirring frequently. Add remaining ¼ cup water; cook 2 to 3 minutes longer, stirring frequently, until vegetables are crisp-tender. Add tofu, orange zest and reserved chili sauce mixture.

5. In measuring cup or small bowl, mix orange juice and cornstarch until blended; add to skillet. Cook and stir until thickened and thoroughly heated. Serve tofu mixture with brown rice.

1 SERVING: CALORIES 420; TOTAL FAT 16G (SATURATED FAT 5G, TRANS FAT 0G); CHOLESTEROL 0MG; SODIUM 980MG; TOTAL CARBOHYDRATE 56G (DIETARY FIBER 9G); PROTEIN 14G **EXCHANGES:** 1½ STARCH, 2 OTHER CARBOHYDRATE, 1 VEGETABLE, 1 VERY LEAN MEAT, 3 FAT **CARBOHYDRATE CHOICES:** 4

Techniques

COOKING WITH TOFU

- Soy beans processed into a solid form, versatile tofu absorbs flavors easily and can be used as a plant-based protein source in meals.
- Tofu is readily available in grocery stores. Look for it in the refrigerated section, as it needs to be kept cold.
- Look for tofu packed in clear liquid with no gelatinous or discolored areas. If the liquid is cloudy, it may be spoiled. When opened, the fresh tofu shouldn't smell or taste sour.
- Check the sell-by date on the package. Unopened, it will keep in the refrigerator 5 days. Once opened, it should be used within 2 days. Store covered with water and change the water daily.
- Tofu can be frozen up 5 months. Freeze in its original container or wrap tightly in plastic wrap.
- Tofu packed in water needs to be drained before cooking. On a plate or other surface, press the tofu between layers of paper towels or kitchen towels, and top with a weight such as a heavy skillet or plate. Let stand at least 1 hour.

STIR-FRY TRICKS

- Stir-frying is quickly cooking small, uniformly sized pieces of usually meat and vegetables in a small amount of oil, helping to retain the crunch and color of the vegetables.
- Woks are great for stir-frying because they allow you to move the foods to the hottest area of the pan (the bottom) or move them away (to the cooler sides), to cook in stages, so all the food will be done at the same time.
- A skillet can be used if you don't have a wok. You'll have to remove some foods from the skillet so that they don't overcook, then add them later to finish the dish.
- Stir-frying takes only minutes, so prepare all your ingredients before you start cooking, allowing you to just toss them into the pan at the appropriate time.
- Cutting each ingredient into the same-size pieces allows them to all get done at the same time.

VARIATIONS ▶

Variations

ORANGE-SESAME NOODLE BOWL
Prepare as directed—except substitute Dutch oven for skillet and omit step 1. Cook 4 ounces thin soba noodles (broken in half) as directed on package; drain. Substitute 3 cups reduced-sodium chicken broth for the water in step 4. Add 2 sliced green onions with the broth. Mix orange juice and cornstarch as directed in step 5. Add to Dutch oven; heat to boiling. Reduce heat; simmer uncovered, stirring constantly, 3 minutes.

ORANGE-SESAME TOFU WITH ASIAN NOODLES
Prepare as directed—except omit step 1. In large stockpot, heat 4 quarts water to boiling over high heat. Remove from heat. Add 7 ounces linguine-style rice stick noodles (from 14-ounce package). Let stand 8 to 10 minutes or until noodles are tender; drain. Add noodles to skillet after heating sauce in step 5; toss to coat.

ORANGE-SESAME TOFU WITH BROCCOLI AND CARROTS
Prepare as directed—except substitute 1 cup ready-to-eat baby-cut carrots, cut lengthwise into ¼-inch strips, for the bell pepper. Top dish with 1 tablespoon toasted sesame seed.

ORANGE-SESAME TOFU WITH CAULIFLOWER AND PEA PODS
Prepare as directed—except substitute cauliflower florets for the broccoli and 1 cup trimmed fresh snow pea pods for the bell pepper. Add the pea pods with the water in step 4.

ORANGE-SESAME TOFU WRAPS
Prepare as directed—except cut tofu into ½-inch cubes. Spoon rice and tofu mixture into large Bibb lettuce leaves.

How to Pull Off
THANKSGIVING DINNER

Use this cheat sheet to make hosting Thanksgiving a breeze! Breaking down the tasks helps your big day go off without a hitch.

2 WEEKS BEFORE
- ☐ Confirm guest list.
- ☐ Assign guests specific dishes to bring.
- ☐ Finalize menu.
- ☐ Plan décor.
- ☐ Purchase frozen turkey.

1 WEEK BEFORE
- ☐ Grocery shop for all nonperishable food items.

3 TO 4 DAYS BEFORE
- ☐ Thaw frozen turkey in refrigerator.
- ☐ Chill white wine and other beverages to serve cold.
- ☐ Purchase perishable food items.

2 DAYS BEFORE
- ☐ Cut vegetables for stuffing and vegetable platter.
- ☐ Prep your favorite green bean casserole except for topping (do not bake). Store in refrigerator.
- ☐ Bake pumpkin or pecan pie (they will hold if made ahead).

1 DAY BEFORE
- ☐ Prep vegetables for side dish.
- ☐ Prep apple or other fruit pie (best baked on day of serving).
- ☐ Set table.

THE BIG DAY
- ☐ Roast the turkey.

WHILE TURKEY ROASTS (ENLIST THE HELP OF GUESTS AND FAMILY)
- ☐ Make and bake stuffing.
- ☐ Top and bake green bean casserole.
- ☐ Make mashed potatoes.
- ☐ Arrange vegetable platter.

WHILE TURKEY RESTS AFTER ROASTING
- ☐ Heat rolls.
- ☐ Make gravy.
- ☐ Make vegetable side dish.
- ☐ Pour beverages.

JUST BEFORE EATING
- ☐ Carve turkey; place on platter and cover to keep warm.
- ☐ Run through menu to make sure all dishes are on the table.

#25 -

One-Pot Mexican
LENTILS, RICE AND BEANS

8 SERVINGS   PREP TIME: **20 MINUTES**   START TO FINISH: **3 HOURS 20 MINUTES**

1   **cup dried black beans (8 oz), sorted, rinsed**

1   **tablespoon vegetable oil**

1   **large onion, chopped (1 cup)**

3   **cloves garlic, finely chopped**

5   **cups vegetable or chicken broth**

1   **tablespoon chili powder**

1½ **teaspoons ground cumin**

1   **teaspoon salt**

½   **teaspoon crushed red pepper flakes**

½   **teaspoon paprika**

1   **cup brown rice**

¾   **cup dried brown lentils (6 oz), sorted, rinsed**

1   **can (4.5 oz) chopped green chiles**

1   **can (28 oz) petite diced tomatoes, undrained**

¼   **cup chopped fresh cilantro**

    Chopped avocado, if desired

    Shredded Cheddar cheese, if desired

1. Soak black beans by one of the methods at right (see Dried Bean Soaking Methods).

2. In 5-quart Dutch oven, heat oil over medium heat. Add onion and garlic; cook 2 to 3 minutes or until onion is soft. Add black beans, broth, chili powder, cumin, salt, pepper flakes and paprika. Heat to boiling. Reduce heat to low; cover and simmer 45 minutes.

3. Add rice, lentils and green chiles. Heat to boiling. Reduce heat to low; cover and simmer, stirring occasionally, about 45 minutes or until rice is tender and lentils are cooked.

4. Stir in tomatoes. Cover and cook 10 to 15 minutes or until hot. Sprinkle with cilantro. Serve with avocado and cheese.

1 SERVING (1½ CUPS): CALORIES 310; TOTAL FAT 3.5G (SATURATED FAT 0.5G, TRANS FAT 0G); CHOLESTEROL 0MG; SODIUM 930MG; TOTAL CARBOHYDRATE 55G (DIETARY FIBER 11G); PROTEIN 14G **EXCHANGES:** 3½ OTHER CARBOHYDRATE, 2 VERY LEAN MEAT, ½ FAT **CARBOHYDRATE CHOICES:** 3½

USING DRIED BEANS

Why start with dried beans when canned beans are so convenient? Dried beans cost about one-third of what canned beans cost. Also, the texture and flavor will be better than with canned beans.

- Before cooking dried beans, sort through them to remove any shriveled, small or damaged beans. Rinse and drain well.
- Dried beans need to be soaked before cooking to soften and plump them. It also removes some of the gas-producing compounds from the dried beans. (Black-eyed peas, lentils and split peas don't have to be soaked before cooking.)
- Dried beans rehydrate to triple their dried size, so choose a pot large enough to cook them with plenty of room for them to expand.

SOAKING METHODS FOR DRIED BEANS

Choose one of these methods for soaking your dried beans prior to cooking:

QUICK-SOAK METHOD: Place dried beans in large saucepan and add enough water to cover. Heat to boiling and boil 2 minutes; remove from heat. Cover and let stand at least 1 hour. Drain.

LONG-SOAK METHOD: Place dried beans in large saucepan or bowl and add enough water to cover. Let stand 8 to 24 hours. Drain.

COOKING DRIED BEANS

Follow directions for cooking dried beans in a specific recipe, or place soaked, drained beans in large saucepan; add enough fresh, cold water to cover. Bring to boil; reduce heat. Cover and simmer, stirring occasionally, for the amount of time specified below.

TYPE OF BEAN (2/3 CUP)	SIMMER TIME	YIELD IN CUPS
Adzuki Beans Lentils	30 to 45 minutes	2 to 3
Mung Beans Split Peas	45 to 60 minutes	2 to 2¼
Black-Eyed Peas, Butter Beans, Cannellini Beans, Great Northern Beans, Lima Beans, Navy Beans, Pinto Beans	1 to 1½ hours	2 to 2½
Anasazi Beans, Black Beans, Fava Beans, Kidney Beans	1 to 2 hours	2
Chick Peas (Garbanzo Beans)	2 to 2½ hours	2
Soybeans	3 to 4 hours	2

VARIATIONS ▶

Variations

MEXICAN LENTIL BURRITOS

Prepare as directed—except cover and refrigerate cooked dish overnight. For each burrito, spoon lentil mixture into large flour tortilla. Sprinkle with shredded Cheddar cheese. Tuck in ends and roll up. Place seam side down on microwavable dinner plate. Microwave uncovered about 1 minute on High or until heated through. Top with additional shredded cheese, sour cream and salsa.

ONE-POT ITALIAN RED LENTILS, RICE AND BEANS

Prepare as directed—except substitute 1 cup dried great northern beans for the black beans and red lentils for the brown lentils. Omit chili powder, cumin and paprika. Add 2 teaspoons dried rosemary leaves and 1 teaspoon dried oregano leaves. Omit green chiles and cilantro. Stir in 3 cups chopped spinach or kale. Substitute grated Parmesan cheese and chopped tomato for the avocado and cheese, if desired.

ONE-POT MEXICAN LENTILS AND CHICKEN

Prepare as directed—except add 2 cups cut-up cooked chicken with the tomatoes.

ONE-POT MEXICAN LENTILS AND SAUSAGE

Prepare as directed—except add ¾ pound cooked smoked sausage, quartered lengthwise and sliced, with the lentils.

SPEEDY ONE-POT MEXICAN LENTILS, RICE AND BEANS

Prepare as directed—except omit step 1. Substitute 2 cans (15 ounces each) black beans, rinsed and drained, for the dried black beans. Reduce broth to 4 cups. Add canned black beans with the tomatoes.

#26

~Family-Favorite
MAC AND CHEESE

6 SERVINGS   PREP TIME: **25 MINUTES**   START TO FINISH: **50 MINUTES**

- **2 cups uncooked elbow macaroni (7 oz)**
- **¼ cup butter**
- **¼ cup all-purpose flour**
- **½ teaspoon salt**
- **¼ teaspoon pepper**
- **¼ teaspoon ground mustard**
- **¼ teaspoon Worcestershire sauce**
- **2 cups milk**
- **2 cups shredded or cubed Cheddar cheese (8 oz)**

1. Heat oven to 350°F. Cook macaroni as directed on package.

2. Meanwhile, melt butter in 3-quart saucepan over low heat. Stir in flour, salt, pepper, mustard and Worcestershire sauce. Increase heat to medium-low and cook, stirring constantly, until mixture is smooth and bubbly; remove from heat. Stir in milk. Heat to boiling, stirring constantly. Boil and stir 1 minute. Stir in cheese. Cook, stirring occasionally, until cheese is melted.

3. Drain macaroni. Gently stir macaroni into cheese sauce. Pour into ungreased 2-quart casserole. Bake uncovered 20 to 25 minutes or until bubbly.

1 SERVING (¾ CUP): CALORIES 420; TOTAL FAT 23G (SATURATED FAT 13G, TRANS FAT 1G); CHOLESTEROL 65MG; SODIUM 670MG; TOTAL CARBOHYDRATE 37G (DIETARY FIBER 2G); PROTEIN 17G **EXCHANGES:** 2 STARCH, ½ LOW-FAT MILK, 1 HIGH-FAT MEAT, 2½ FAT **CARBOHYDRATE CHOICES:** 2½

TEST KITCHEN TIP

Mac and cheese thickens as it cools, so be sure to serve it immediately after baking. If you are lucky enough to have leftovers, reheat with a tablespoon or two of milk, stirring freqently to make it creamy again.

MAKING A ROUX

The key to legendary mac and cheese is making a velvety-smooth cheese sauce by starting with a roux. It only takes a few minutes, but it's necessary to creating a successful sauce.

- A roux is a mixture of flour and fat (usually butter) that's cooked until bubbly and smooth, and it's used to thicken liquids into a sauce.
- The butter is melted first so that it can coat the flour, which prevents lumps from forming when the liquid is added.
- Cook and stir the mixture constantly to avoid burning and to prevent lumps from forming. A whisk works well, but be sure to scrape along the entire bottom of the pan and where the side of the pan meets the bottom.
- It's important to use the temperature and cook time specified in the recipe to avoid either burning the mixture or over- or undercooking the roux and sauce, which can cause the sauce to have the wrong thickness.
- Cooking the mixture for a minute after adding the liquid ensures that the flour taste has been cooked out and that the mixture has had enough time to thicken.

VARIATIONS ▶

Variations

BACON AND BROCCOLI MAC AND CHEESE
Prepare as directed—except stir 1½ cups finely chopped broccoli florets into the cheese sauce with the macaroni in step 3. Top with 3 slices crisply cooked and crumbled bacon before baking.

BUFFALO CHICKEN MAC AND CHEESE
Prepare as directed—except stir 3 to 4 tablespoons Buffalo wing sauce into the cheese sauce in step 2. Stir in 1½ cups cut-up cooked chicken with the macaroni in step 3. Immediately after baking, sprinkle macaroni and cheese with ¼ cup finely chopped celery and ⅓ cup crumbled blue cheese.

CRISPY-TOPPED MAC AND CHEESE
Prepare as directed—except while macaroni and cheese is baking, heat 2 teaspoons olive or vegetable oil in 8-inch skillet over medium heat. Add ¼ cup Italian-style panko crispy bread crumbs. Cook 2 to 3 minutes, stirring constantly, until golden brown; remove from heat. Before serving, sprinkle bread crumbs over macaroni.

HOT DOG MAC AND CHEESE
Prepare as directed—except while stirring the cooked macaroni into the cheese sauce, add slices of hot dog or bite-size pieces of cooked sausage.

MEXICAN MAC AND CHEESE
Prepare as directed—except substitute shredded pepper Jack cheese for the Cheddar cheese and stir 1 can (10 ounces) drained diced tomatoes with green chiles into the cheese sauce in step 2.

BASIC OMELET

4 OMELETS   PREP TIME: **40 MINUTES**   START TO FINISH: **40 MINUTES**

8   eggs

    Salt and pepper, if desired

8   **teaspoons butter**

1. For each omelet, in small bowl, beat 2 eggs until fluffy. Add salt and pepper to taste. In 8-inch nonstick omelet pan or skillet, heat 2 teaspoons butter over medium-high heat just until butter is hot and sizzling. As butter melts, tilt pan to coat bottom.

2. Quickly pour eggs into pan. While rapidly sliding pan back and forth over heat, quickly and continuously stir with spatula to spread eggs over bottom of pan as they thicken. Let stand over heat a few seconds to lightly brown bottom of omelet. Do not overcook; omelet will continue to cook after folding. If desired, add filling before folding.

3. To remove from pan, first run spatula under one edge of omelet, folding about one-third of it to the center. Transfer to plate by tilting pan, letting flat unfolded edge of omelet slide out onto plate. Using edge of pan as a guide, flip folded edge of omelet over flat portion on plate.

4. Repeat with remaining eggs and butter. If desired, omelets can be kept warm on heatproof platter in 200°F oven while preparing remaining omelets.

1 OMELET: CALORIES 220; TOTAL FAT 18G (SATURATED FAT 7G, TRANS FAT 0G); CHOLESTEROL 445MG; SODIUM 170MG; TOTAL CARBOHYDRATE 1G (DIETARY FIBER 0G); PROTEIN 13G **EXCHANGES:** 2 MEDIUM-FAT MEAT, 1½ FAT **CARBOHYDRATE CHOICES:** 0

"EGGS-TRAORDINARY" OMELETS

Omelets are the ultimate customizable dish! They are best made individually and served immediately. You can customize each omelet to personal tastes if you like.

- Omelets take just minutes to cook, so before cooking them, have any filling ingredients prepped and ready to add as directed—either with the egg mixture or folded into the omelet before serving.
- Omelet pans are shallow and sloped to make it easy to move the eggs around, cook them and slip the omelet out easily. If you don't have one, choose a skillet with sloping sides for the best results.
- If the technique of folding the omelet into thirds with the help of the pan is mystifying, simply place any omelet fillings on one half of the cooked omelet, fold the other half over the filling and then lift the omelet out of the pan onto the serving plate.

Quickly and continuously stir eggs with spatula to spread eggs over bottom of pan as they thicken.

To remove from pan, first run spatula under one side of omelet.

Fold ⅓ of omelet over center.

Transfer to plate by titlting pan, using edge of pan to slide omelet onto plate.

VARIATIONS ▶

Variations

CHEESE OMELET
Prepare as directed—except before folding each omelet, sprinkle with ¼ cup shredded Cheddar, Monterey Jack or Swiss cheese or ¼ cup crumbled blue cheese.

CHEESY VEGETABLE OMELET
Prepare as directed—except before cooking omelets, heat 2 teaspoons olive or vegetable oil in pan. Stir in 1 cup chopped broccoli and ½ cup chopped bell pepper (any color) and cook about 3 minutes. Add ½ cup chopped tomato; cook and stir 1 minute longer. Remove from pan; reserve. Before folding omelet, sprinkle with 2 tablespoons shredded Monterey Jack cheese and some of reserved veggies.

DENVER OMELET
Prepare as directed—except before adding eggs to pan, for each omelet cook 2 tablespoons chopped cooked ham, 1 tablespoon finely chopped bell pepper and 1 tablespoon finely chopped onion in butter about 2 minutes, stirring frequently. Continue as directed in step 2.

HAM AND CHEESE OMELET
Prepare as directed—except before folding each omelet, sprinkle with 2 tablespoons shredded Cheddar, Monterey Jack or Swiss cheese and 2 tablespoons finely chopped cooked ham.

SWEET BERRY-ALMOND OMELET
Prepare as directed—except omit bell pepper. Add 2 tablespoons sugar with the salt. When each omelet is cooked, spread with 2 tablespoons strawberry preserves. Top with scant ¼ cup sliced fresh strawberries and 1 tablespoon toasted sliced almonds. Continue as directed in step 3. Sprinkle powdered sugar lightly over omelet on plate.

28

Cheesy Broccoli
FRITTATA

4 SERVINGS   PREP TIME: **15 MINUTES**   START TO FINISH: **25 MINUTES**

4   **eggs**

¼   **cup milk**

1   **tablespoon chopped fresh parsley**

¼   **teaspoon salt**

¼   **teaspoon red pepper sauce**

1   **tablespoon vegetable oil**

1   **cup broccoli florets**

1   **medium carrot, shredded (½ cup)**

1   **medium onion, chopped (½ cup)**

1   **cup shredded Cheddar cheese (4 oz)**

1   **tablespoon grated Parmesan cheese**

1. In medium bowl, beat eggs, milk, parsley, salt and pepper sauce with whisk until well blended; set aside.

2. In 10-inch nonstick skillet, heat oil over medium-high heat. Cook broccoli, carrot and onion in oil about 5 minutes, stirring frequently, until vegetables are crisp-tender.

3. Pour egg mixture over vegetables. Sprinkle with cheeses; reduce heat to low. Cover; cook about 10 minutes or until eggs are set in center. Cut into 4 wedges.

1 SERVING: CALORIES 260; TOTAL FAT 19G (SATURATED FAT 8G, TRANS FAT 0G); CHOLESTEROL 220MG; SODIUM 450MG; TOTAL CARBOHYDRATE 7G (DIETARY FIBER 1G); PROTEIN 15G **EXCHANGES:** ½ OTHER CARBOHYDRATE, 1 MEDIUM-FAT MEAT, 1 HIGH-FAT MEAT, 1 FAT **CARBOHYDRATE CHOICES:** ½

TEST KITCHEN TIP

Get a jump on meals by prepping ingredients when you have a few minutes to spare. Chop veggies; place in covered containers or resealable bags and refrigerate. Ingredients that will be used together in the same step can be stored together.

COOKING FRITTATAS

- Fillings should be cooked before adding the eggs, so cook ingredients such as veggies, shrimp and chicken in the skillet first, or start with fillings that have already been cooked.
- Filling ingredients should be bite-size or smaller so that the eggs can cook evenly and the frittata can be removed easily from the skillet and cut.
- Use whatever filling ingredients you have on hand. Mix and match fresh herbs, cooked meat, chicken and seafood, veggies, cheese and grains for a different frittata every time.

REMOVING AND SERVING FRITTATAS

- Be sure to use a nonstick skillet so that your frittata can slip out of the pan easily.
- The easiest way to serve frittatas is cut into wedges, right out of the skillet. You can also slip the whole frittata onto a serving platter or invert it onto the serving platter to show off the beautiful golden-brown bottom.
- Frittatas are also great cold. Bring them to a picnic, or take leftovers to work for a satisfying homemade lunch.

VARIATIONS ▶

Variations

ARTICHOKE AND BASIL FRITTATA

Prepare as directed—except omit broccoli, carrot and Cheddar cheese. Substitute red onion for the onion and add 2 cloves finely chopped garlic and 2 tablespoons chopped fresh basil leaves with the onion. Cook onion mixture 3 minutes or until onion is tender. Arrange 1 can (14 ounces) artichoke hearts, drained and quartered, over eggs after adding them to the pan in step 3. Sprinkle with 2 tablespoons grated Parmesan cheese.

CANADIAN BACON–POTATO FRITTATA

Prepare as directed—except add 2 tablespoons chopped fresh chives and ⅛ teaspoon dried thyme leaves with the pepper sauce. Omit vegetable oil, broccoli, carrot and onion. Spray skillet with cooking spray; heat pan over medium heat. Cook and stir ¼ cup chopped bell pepper in pan 1 minute. Add 1½ cups frozen southern-style hash-brown potatoes. Cover and cook, stirring frequently, 8 to 10 minutes or until potatoes begin to brown. Stir in ⅓ cup coarsely chopped Canadian bacon; cook and stir 1 to 2 minutes or until heated. Continue as directed in step 3.

CARAMELIZED ONION–PANCETTA FRITTATA

Prepare as directed—except omit vegetable oil, broccoli, carrot, onion and Cheddar cheese. Cook 4 ounces chopped pancetta (Italian-style bacon) in skillet over medium heat 8 to 10 minutes or until crisp. Drain on paper towels; return to skillet. Stir in Caramelized Onions (page 46). Pour eggs over onion mixture; sprinkle with 2 ounces chèvre (goat) cheese, crumbled (½ cup). Cook as directed in step 3. Crumble an additional 2 ounces chèvre (goat) cheese (½ cup) and ¼ cup hredded Parmesan cheese over frittata before serving.

CORN AND SALSA FRITTATA

Prepare as directed—except stir ⅓ cup salsa and ⅛ teaspoon garlic powder in with the eggs; stir in 1 cup drained whole kernel corn with red and green peppers (from 11-ounce can) and 1 can (4.5 ounces) undrained chopped green chiles. Omit vegetable oil, broccoli, carrot and onion. Continue as directed in step 3. Top cooked frittata with additional salsa and sliced ripe olives. Serve with sour cream.

SAUSAGE-CHEESE FRITTATA

Prepare as directed—except omit vegetable oil, broccoli and carrot. Cook ½ pound bulk hot Italian pork sausage and the onion in skillet over medium-high heat 10 minutes, stirring frequently, until no longer pink; drain. Continue as directed in step 3.

IRRESISTIBLE

Sides

#29

~Fabulous~
OVEN FRIES

4 SERVINGS   PREP TIME: **15 MINUTES**   START TO FINISH: **45 MINUTES**

2 lb russet potatoes (about 2 large)

½ teaspoon salt

¼ teaspoon pepper

1. Heat oven to 450°F. Generously spray 2 baking pans with cooking spray. Cut potatoes lengthwise into quarters. Cut quarters lengthwise into ¼-inch-wide slices. Place potatoes in 1-gallon resealable food-storage plastic bag.

2. Add salt and pepper to bag; seal. Shake vigorously until potatoes are coated.

3. Divide potatoes between baking pans in single layer; spray with cooking spray. Bake 15 minutes; turn potatoes and rotate pans. Bake 10 to 15 minutes longer or until golden brown.

1 SERVING: CALORIES 180; TOTAL FAT 0G (SATURATED FAT 0G, TRANS FAT 0G); CHOLESTEROL 0MG; SODIUM 310MG; TOTAL CARBOHYDRATE 39G (DIETARY FIBER 4G); PROTEIN 4G **EXCHANGES:** ½ STARCH, 2 OTHER CARBOHYDRATE, ½ VEGETABLE **CARBOHYDRATE CHOICES:** 2½

TEST KITCHEN TIP

If you have a convection oven, use it for this recipe! The warm circulating air will help to dry out the surfaces of the potatoes, making them crispier. Use the same oven temperature as for a regular oven.

Techniques

CHOOSING AND PREPARING POTATOES

- Choose starchy potatoes such as russet or Idaho potatoes for oven fries that are crispy on the outside and tender on the inside.
- Cut the potatoes into narrow strips, as directed, for the best texture inside and out. They are thin enough to crisp up on the outside and cook through at the same time.
- If they are cut too thin, the edges can burn before the insides are cooked. Too thick, and the fries won't get crispy.

MAXIMIZE THE CRISPY EXTERIORS

- Using a high oven temperature helps to evaporate enough moisture from the surface of the potatoes to make them crispy.
- Spraying the pan and fries with cooking spray helps them crisp up and brown.
- Dividing the potatoes between two pans gives them enough exposure to the hot oven temperature to make the edges crispy.
- Serving the fries immediately keeps the steam inside the potatoes from softening the crispy exteriors.

HOW CRISPY?

Oven fries aren't quite as crispy as deep-fried French fries, but if the tips above are followed, the difference in texture is minimal and worth the ease of preparation and savings in calories and fat compared to deep-fried potatoes.

VARIATIONS ▶

Variations

BASIL-PARMESAN OVEN FRIES

Prepare as directed—except omit pepper. Place potato strips in large bowl. Spray generously with cooking spray; toss to coat. Sprinkle with ¼ cup grated Parmesan cheese, 1 tablespoon dried basil leaves, the salt and ¼ teaspoon garlic powder.

GARLIC-PEPPER OVEN FRIES

Prepare as directed—except omit pepper. Place potato strips in large bowl. Spray generously with cooking spray; toss to coat. Sprinkle with 3 cloves finely chopped garlic, the salt and 1 teaspoon cracked pepper.

SEASONED FRIES

Prepare as directed—except substitute 1 teaspoon seasoned salt and 2 teaspoons finely chopped fresh rosemary or ½ teaspoon dried rosemary leaves for the salt and pepper.

SWEET-AND-SPICY SWEET POTATO FRIES

Prepare as directed—except substitute sweet potatoes for the russet potatoes. Add 1 teaspoon ground cumin and 1 teaspoon chili powder with the salt and pepper in bag. (Sweet potatoes may not become as crispy as the russets.)

ZESTY DIPPING SAUCE FOR FRIES

For a quick dipping sauce, stir 2 tablespoons barbecue sauce into ½ cup sour cream.

#30

Creamy
POTATO SALAD

10 SERVINGS   PREP TIME: **20 MINUTES**   START TO FINISH: **5 HOURS**

6   medium unpeeled round red or Yukon Gold potatoes (2 lb)

1½   cups mayonnaise or salad dressing

1   tablespoon white or cider vinegar

1   tablespoon yellow mustard

1   teaspoon salt

¼   teaspoon pepper

2   medium stalks celery, chopped (1 cup)

⅓   cup chopped onion

2   tablespoons chopped green onions (2 medium)

4   hard-cooked eggs, chopped

    Paprika, if desired

1. In 3-quart saucepan, place potatoes and just enough water to cover potatoes. Cover and heat to boiling; reduce heat to low.

2. Cook 30 to 35 minutes or until potatoes are tender when pierced with fork; drain. Let stand until cool enough to handle. Peel potatoes; cut into cubes.

3. In large glass or plastic bowl, mix mayonnaise, vinegar, mustard, salt and pepper. Add potatoes, celery, onion and green onion; toss. Stir in eggs. Sprinkle with paprika. Cover and refrigerate at least 4 hours to chill and blend flavors.

1 SERVING (½ CUP): CALORIES 330; TOTAL FAT 27G (SATURATED FAT 4.5G, TRANS FAT 0G); CHOLESTEROL 90MG; SODIUM 490MG; TOTAL CARBOHYDRATE 18G (DIETARY FIBER 2G); PROTEIN 4G **EXCHANGES:** 1 STARCH, 5½ FAT **CARBOHYDRATE CHOICES:** 1

TEST KITCHEN TIP

What's to your taste? Salad dressing will give potato salad a tangier, sweeter flavor that's slightly more pronounced than if you prepare potato salad with mayonnaise, which is more mild and just contributes creaminess.

Techniques

CHOOSING POTATOES

- All-purpose potatoes such as Yukon Gold or waxy potatoes such as fingerling, new or red potatoes work the best for potato salad.
- Starchy potatoes such as russet or Idaho tend to fall apart during cooking.
- We chose Yukon Gold or red potatoes for their similar size and therefore similar cooking time. If you use one of the other suggested varieties, you may need to increase or decrease the cooking time.

COOKING POTATOES

- Cut potatoes into same-size pieces so they all will be done at the same time. If potatoes aren't cooked long enough, you'll end up with tiny lumps of hard potatoes throughout your mashed potatoes.
- Start the potatoes in cool tap water so that they can cook evenly all the way through.
- Potatoes are tender when you can easily poke them to the center with a paring knife.
- Cook potatoes just until they are tender. If not cooked enough, the potatoes will be unappealingly crunchy; cooked too long, they can become mushy and fall apart.
- Peeling potatoes is a breeze when they are cooked—the skins will slip right off.

MAKING POTATO SALAD

- Be sure to allow the potatoes to cool only long enough to make them easy to handle.
- Potatoes will soak up the flavors of the dressing and seasoning much better if added while warm.
- Chill the potato salad at least 4 hours so the flavors have enough time to blend for the best-tasting salad.

VARIATIONS ▶

Variations

BLT POTATO SALAD
Prepare as directed—except add 1 tablespoon chopped fresh dill weed with the onion. Toss potato salad with ¾ cup cherry tomato halves, 1½ cups bite-size pieces romaine lettuce and 4 slices crisply cooked and crumbled bacon before refrigerating.

GREEN BEAN POTATO SALAD
Prepare as directed—except substitute 1 cup 1-inch pieces cooked and drained fresh or frozen green beans for the celery.

HERB VINAIGRETTE POTATO SALAD
Prepare as directed—except omit mayonnaise, vinegar, mustard and pepper. Increase salt to 1½ teaspoons. In step 3, mix ½ cup vegetable oil, ¼ cup fresh lemon juice, ¼ cup chopped fresh basil leaves, 2 tablespoons each chopped fresh parsley and thyme leaves and the salt. Continue as directed.

PEAS AND CHEESE POTATO SALAD
Prepare as directed—except add 1 cup frozen sweet peas during the last minute of cooking time with the potatoes. Substitute 1 cup finely diced Cheddar cheese for the celery.

SOUTHWEST POTATO SALAD
Prepare as directed—except omit vinegar, mustard and pepper. Reduce salt to ½ teaspoon. In step 3, mix mayonnaise with 2½ tablespoons milk, 1¼ teaspoons cumin seed, 1 or 2 finely chopped chipotle chiles in adobo sauce (from 7-ounce can) and the salt. Substitute 1 cup chopped red bell pepper for the celery and ½ cup sliced green onions for the onion.

MASHED POTATOES

6 SERVINGS   PREP TIME: **10 MINUTES**   START TO FINISH: **40 MINUTES**

6 medium round red, white, Yukon Gold or russet potatoes (2 lb), peeled if desired, cut into quarters

⅓ to ½ cup milk, warmed

¼ cup butter, softened

½ teaspoon salt

Dash pepper

Additional butter, cut into small pieces, if desired

Paprika, if desired

Chopped fresh parsley, if desired

Chopped fresh chives, if desired

1. In 2-quart saucepan, place potatoes and enough water just to cover potatoes. Heat to boiling; reduce heat. Cover and simmer 20 to 30 minutes or until potatoes are tender when pierced with fork; drain. Shake pan with potatoes over low heat to dry them.

2. Mash potatoes in pan with potato masher until no lumps remain. Add milk in small amounts, mashing after each addition.

3. Add butter, salt and pepper. Mash vigorously until potatoes are light and fluffy and desired consistency. Dot with small pieces of butter or sprinkle with paprika, chopped fresh parsley or chives.

1 SERVING: CALORIES 200; TOTAL FAT 8G (SATURATED FAT 4G, TRANS FAT 0G); CHOLESTEROL 20MG; SODIUM 260MG; TOTAL CARBOHYDRATE 28G (DIETARY FIBER 3G); PROTEIN 3G **EXCHANGES:** 1 STARCH, 1 OTHER CARBOHYDRATE, 1½ FAT **CARBOHYDRATE CHOICES:** 2

Techniques

PREPARING POTATOES

See Cooking Potatoes (page 143).

MAKING MASHED POTATOES

- Cut potatoes into same-size pieces so all pieces of the pieces will be tender at the same time.
- Shake the pan with the potatoes over low heat after draining to remove more water from the potatoes, which will make them fluffier.
- Before adding any additional ingredients, mash the potatoes with a potato masher until no lumps remain.
- By adding the milk in small amounts at a time, rather than all at once, you can control the texture of the potatoes so they don't become runny.
- The amount of milk needed for the mashed potatoes will depend on the type of potato used.
- Use warm milk to keep your potatoes warm. You can heat the milk in a microwavable glass measure 10 to 30 seconds on High or until warm.

Variations

BUTTERMILK MASHED POTATOES: Prepare as directed—except substitute warm buttermilk for the milk.

CHEESY MASHED POTATOES: Prepare as directed—except stir in 1 cup (4 ounces) shredded cheese (Asiago, Cheddar, Monterey Jack or Parmesan) or crumbled cheese (blue or Gorgonzola) with the butter, salt and pepper in step 3.

CHIPOTLE-CHEDDAR MASHED POTATOES: Prepare as directed—except stir in 1 cup shredded Cheddar cheese (4 ounces) and 1 to 2 chipotle chiles in adobo sauce (from 7-ounce can), finely chopped, with the butter, salt and pepper in step 3.

GARLIC MASHED POTATOES: Prepare as directed—except add 6 cloves garlic, peeled, with the potatoes in step 1. Mash garlic with potatoes.

MASHED POTATO BOWLS: Prepare as directed—except spoon leftover mashed potatoes into microwavable serving bowls. Top with leftover cooked meat or seafood, such as cut-up cooked chicken or taco meat or cooked shrimp. Add cooked veggies, such as corn, broccoli, cauliflower or green beans. Add shredded cheese and a sauce, such as gravy or cheese sauce. Cover with plastic wrap and heat about 1 minute on High or until hot. Sprinkle with sliced green onions, chopped fresh cilantro or chopped green chiles, if desired.

FLUFFY RICE

14 SERVINGS   PREP TIME: **10 MINUTES**   START TO FINISH: **30 MINUTES**

2   **tablespoons butter**

2   **cups long-grain white rice**

½   **teaspoon salt**

4   **cups Slow-Cooker Chicken Bone Broth (page 69) or canned chicken broth**

1. In 3-quart saucepan, melt butter over medium heat. Add rice; cook 2 to 4 minutes, stirring occasionally, until rice has absorbed butter and is lightly toasted.

2. Add salt and broth to saucepan. Heat to boiling; reduce heat. Cover and simmer 10 to 15 minutes or until liquid is absorbed and rice is tender. Remove from heat, let stand 5 minutes. Fluff with a fork. Serve immediately.

1 SERVING (½ CUP): CALORIES 120; TOTAL FAT 2G (SATURATED FAT 1G, TRANS FAT 0G); CHOLESTEROL 0MG; SODIUM 330MG; TOTAL CARBOHYDRATE 23G (DIETARY FIBER 0G); PROTEIN 2G **EXCHANGES:** ½ STARCH, 1 OTHER CARBOHYDRATE, ½ FAT **CARBOHYDRATE CHOICES:** 1½

FLUFFY BAKED RICE

Heat oven to 425°F. Spray 13x9-inch (3-quart) glass baking dish with cooking spray. In 3-quart saucepan, bring 5 cups chicken bone broth to boil. Remove from heat; set aside. Pour rice evenly into baking dish; sprinkle with salt. Pour hot broth over rice. Cover baking dish with foil. Bake 20 to 25 minutes. Let stand 10 minutes until all liquid is absorbed; remove foil. Fluff with fork.

COOKING RICE

- In general, heat the rice, liquid and seasonings to boiling, and then reduce the heat to just barely simmering so that the rice can cook slowly.
- Other types of rice may be substituted for the white rice. See Timetable for Cooking Rice (below) for specific directions.
- Water can be used to cook rice, or you can add flavor to your rice by using broth. We call for Slow-Cooker Chicken Bone Broth to be used for extra flavor and nutrients, but canned broth can be used as well.
- Other seasonings can be added to vary the flavor of the rice. Consider adding sautéed mushrooms, garlic or onions, dried or fresh herbs, or lemon or lime zest to the rice with the salt and broth.
- Another way to add flavor is to toast the rice before cooking it. Melt 2 tablespoons butter in pan over medium heat; add rice. Cook 2 to 4 minutes, stirring occasionally, or until rice is lightly toasted. (The rice may look golden brown, depending on the variety, or it will smell toasted.) Add liquid and salt and continue as directed.
- Keep the pan covered with a tight-fitting lid. If the lid isn't tight, water or broth can escape as steam, robbing the rice of the moisture it needs to cook through. Check the rice occasionally to be sure the liquid is at a low simmer and hasn't completely disappeared. Add a tablespoon or two of additional water if the bottom of the pan is dry.
- Let the cooked rice rest. When the rice is tender and almost all of the liquid has disappeared, remove the pan from the heat and let stand covered for 5 to 10 minutes. The rice will continue to absorb the liquid. Uncover and fluff the rice with a fork just before serving.
- Rice is easy to cook in large batches and store for quick meals anytime. Use leftover rice in burritos, soups, stews, salads or rice bowls. Store cooked rice tightly covered in the refrigerator up to 5 days or freeze up to 3 months.

TIMETABLE FOR COOKING RICE

TYPE OF RICE (1 CUP)	AMOUNT OF WATER IN CUPS	COOKING DIRECTIONS	YIELD IN CUPS
Basmati White	1½	Simmer 15 to 20 minutes.	3
Jasmine	1¾	Simmer 15 to 20 minutes.	3
Long-Grain White	2	Simmer 20 to 25 minutes	3
Parboiled (Converted) White	2½	Simmer 20 minutes. Let stand 5 minutes.	3 to 4
Precooked (Instant) White	1	After stirring in rice, cover and remove from heat; let stand 5 minutes.	2
Long-Grain Brown (Regular and Basmati)	2¾	Simmer 45 to 50 minutes.	4
Precooked (Instant) Brown	1½	Simmer 10 minutes.	2
Wild	2½	Simmer 40 to 50 minutes.	3

VARIATIONS ▶

Variations

CILANTRO-LIME RICE

Prepare as directed—except substitute jasmine rice for the long-grain rice. Cook 2 minced cloves garlic with rice. Increase bone broth to 3 cups. Add 2 tablespoons fresh lime juice with the salt. Cook 15 minutes. Stir in ⅓ cup chopped fresh cilantro and ½ finely chopped green onion. Remove from heat; let stand 5 minutes. Fluff with fork.

JASMINE-LEMON RICE PILAF

Prepare as directed—except substitute olive oil for the butter and jasmine rice for the long-grain rice. In 10-inch nonstick skillet, heat oil over medium heat. Add jasmine rice, 1 finely chopped clove garlic and ½ cup chopped onion. Cook 2 to 4 minutes, stirring frequently, until rice absorbs oil and is lightly toasted. Increase bone broth to 3 cups. Add ¼ teaspoon pepper with the salt. Stir 1 teaspoon grated lemon zest, 1 tablespoon fresh lemon juice, 2 tablespoons chopped fresh Italian (flat-leaf) parsley and 1 tablespoon chopped fresh basil into the hot rice.

MEXICAN CHEESY RICE

Prepare as directed—except add 1 to 2 tablespoons chopped green pickled sliced jalapeños, drained (from 12-ounce can), with the bone broth. Immediately after cooking, sprinkle rice with ½ cup shredded Colby–Monterey Jack cheese. Remove from heat; let stand 5 minutes. Fluff with fork.

MUSHROOM RICE WITH THYME

Prepare as directed—except before cooking rice, in 10-inch skillet, heat 1 tablespoon each butter and vegetable oil, and ¼ teaspoon each salt, pepper and dried thyme leaves over medium-high heat until butter is melted. Stir in 8 ounces sliced button mushrooms. Cook 4 to 6 minutes, stirring occasionally, until mushrooms are tender. Transfer cooked mushrooms to saucepan; add rice, broth and salt. Continue as directed.

RICE PILAF

Prepare as directed—except before cooking rice, melt butter in pan over medium heat. Cook ⅓ cup chopped onion (1 small) in butter about 3 minutes, stirring occasionally, until tender. Stir in rice. Cook 2 to 4 minutes, stirring occasionally, until lightly toasted. Add broth and salt to pan. Continue as directed.

#33   BREAD STUFFING

10 SERVINGS   PREP TIME: **15 MINUTES**   START TO FINISH: **55 MINUTES**

¾   cup butter

2   large stalks celery (with leaves), chopped (1½ cups)

1   large onion, chopped (1 cup)

9   cups soft bread cubes (about 15 slices bread)

1½   teaspoons chopped fresh or ½ teaspoon dried thyme leaves

1½   teaspoons chopped fresh or ½ teaspoon dried sage leaves or ¼ teaspoon ground sage

1   teaspoon salt

¼   teaspoon pepper

1. Heat oven to 350°F. Spray 13x9-inch (3-quart) glass baking dish with cooking spray.

2. In 4-quart Dutch oven or saucepan, melt butter over medium-high heat. Cook celery and onion in butter 4 to 6 minutes, stirring occasionally, until tender. Add remaining ingredients; stir gently to mix well. Spoon into baking dish.

3. Cover with foil; bake 25 minutes. Remove foil; bake 10 to 15 minutes longer or until center is hot and edges are beginning to brown.

1 SERVING (½ CUP): CALORIES 230; TOTAL FAT 15G (SATURATED FAT 7G, TRANS FAT 1G); CHOLESTEROL 35MG; SODIUM 530MG; TOTAL CARBOHYDRATE 19G (DIETARY FIBER 1G); PROTEIN 3G **EXCHANGES:** 1 STARCH, 3 FAT **CARBOHYDRATE CHOICES:** 1

Techniques

PREPARING STUFFING

Stuffing is a delicious side dish any time of year. You don't need to roast a turkey to make it.

STUFFING FOOD SAFELY

- For optimal food safety and even doneness, the USDA recommends cooking stuffing separately from the bird because the stuffing itself needs to reach 165°F; by the time it would, your turkey could be overcooked and dry.
- If you choose to stuff your turkey, chicken or game birds, it is necessary to use an accurate food thermometer to make sure the center of the stuffing reaches 165°F. Bacteria from the raw poultry juice can survive in stuffing if it hasn't reached that temperature.

CUSTOMIZING YOUR STUFFING

You can customize stuffing by using whatever type of bread, sautéed vegetables, seasonings and liquid you like:

- Pick a bread that won't fall apart when lightly moistened. Day-old bread can be used, but you'll need more liquid than if using soft bread cubes.
- Grains such as wild rice, barley or quinoa can be used instead of bread, but you won't need as much liquid.
- Sauté vegetables until they are tender if you like soft stuffing or until crisp-tender if you like a bit of crunch in your stuffing.
- Add protein such as cooked sausage, hot Italian sausage, chorizo or sage pork sausage. Or add cooked bacon or pancetta or seafood, such as oysters.
- Add fresh or dried herbs. Sage is the quintessential herb for stuffing, but also consider adding parsley, thyme or rosemary (use sparingly).
- Add or use other seasonings such as pepper, chili powder or crushed red pepper flakes or smoked paprika.
- Keep your stuffing light on salt because adding butter or chicken broth will increase the saltiness. Those who enjoy gravy over the stuffing will find it saltier yet. Using reduced-sodium broth and limiting the amount of added salt will help keep the sodium in check.
- Add interest with nuts, seeds or dried fruit such as dried cranberries, cherries or raisins.

STUFFING KNOW-HOW

Add enough liquid to make your stuffing moist but not soggy. Too much liquid and the bread cubes will fall apart and create a sticky mush. Too little liquid and the stuffing will be dry.

Pack stuffing lightly in the baking dish—don't stuff the dish! Stuffing can expand while cooking; packing it lightly keeps the texture intact.

Bake stuffing covered at first and then uncovered to allow the top and edges to begin to brown and get crisp.

VARIATIONS ▶

Cornbread Stuffing

Oyster Stuffing

Wild Rice Stuffing

Bread Stuffing

BREAD STUFFING (CONTINUED)

Variations

CORNBREAD STUFFING
Prepare as directed—except substitute cornbread cubes for the soft bread cubes.

CORNBREAD-SAUSAGE STUFFING
Prepare as directed—except omit salt. Add ½ pound cooked crumbled bulk pork or chorizo sausage (see Sausage Stuffing below) and 1 cup chopped toasted pecans with the remaining stuffing ingredients.

GIBLET STUFFING
Prepare as directed—except place giblets and neck—but not liver—from turkey or chicken in 2-quart saucepan. Add enough water to cover; season with salt and pepper. Simmer uncovered over low heat 1 to 2 hours or until tender; drain. Remove meat from neck and finely chop with giblets. Add with the remaining stuffing ingredients.

OYSTER STUFFING
Prepare as directed—except add 2 cans (8 ounces each) whole oysters, drained and chopped, with the remaining stuffing ingredients.

SAUSAGE STUFFING
Prepare as directed—except omit salt. In 10-inch skillet, cook 1 pound bulk pork sausage or fresh chorizo sausage over medium heat, stirring occasionally, until no longer pink; drain, reserving drippings. Substitute drippings for part of the butter. Add cooked sausage with the remaining stuffing ingredients.

WILD RICE STUFFING
Prepare as directed—except in ungreased 2-quart casserole, mix 3 cups cooked wild rice, ¼ cup melted butter, 1 cup fresh orange juice, 1 medium apple, peeled and cut into chunks, 1 cup dry bread crumbs and ½ cup each raisins and walnuts. Cover and bake at 325°F 55 to 60 minutes or until apple is tender.

ROASTED VEGETABLES

10 SERVINGS   PREP TIME: **15 MINUTES**   START TO FINISH: **40 MINUTES**

- **3**   **tablespoons olive or vegetable oil**
- **½**   **teaspoon salt**
- **⅛**   **teaspoon pepper**
- **1**   **clove garlic, finely chopped**
- **1**   **cup ready-to-eat baby-cut carrots**
- **6**   **small red potatoes, cut into quarters**
- **2**   **small onions, cut into ½-inch wedges**
- **1**   **small red bell pepper, cut into 1-inch pieces**
- **1**   **medium zucchini, cut lengthwise in half, then cut crosswise into 1-inch slices**
- **1**   **cup grape or cherry tomatoes**

1. Heat oven to 450°F. In small bowl, stir oil, salt, pepper and garlic until well mixed. In ungreased 15x10x1-inch pan, toss carrots, potatoes, onions, bell pepper and zucchini with oil mixture until coated.

2. Roast uncovered 20 minutes, stirring once. Stir in tomatoes. Roast about 5 minutes longer or until vegetables are tender and starting to brown.

1 SERVING: CALORIES 110; TOTAL FAT 4.5G (SATURATED FAT 0.5G, TRANS FAT 0G); CHOLESTEROL 0MG; SODIUM 130MG; TOTAL CARBOHYDRATE 16G (DIETARY FIBER 3G); PROTEIN 2G **EXCHANGES:** ½ STARCH, 1 VEGETABLE, 1 FAT **CARBOHYDRATE CHOICES:** 1

TEST KITCHEN TIP

Enlist your convection oven! The circulating heat helps to dry out and caramelize the edges of the veggies for a great flavor.

Techniques

WHY ROAST?

- Crispy and browned on the outside, tender on the inside, roasting veggies causes the sugars in them to caramelize, heightening and sweetening their flavors.
- Roasting is an easy method for cooking veggies that requires little prep or attention while cooking.
- Roasting is done at temperatures higher than 400°F to achieve the dual textures. If veggies are cooked at lower temperatures, you won't get the caramelized outsides—they'll just get soft all over.

TIPS FOR ROASTING

- Cut veggies in similar-size pieces so that they will be done at the same time.
- Toss veggies with a small amount of olive or vegetable oil, and season before cooking.
- Use a large enough pan so that the vegetables can be in a single layer and have a little room around them.
- Use a short-sided pan, such as a 15x10x1 inch or shallow roasting pan, to allow the moisture in the veggies to evaporate quickly so they will roast rather than steam.
- Individual recipes will provide specific directions, but in general, cook veggies until crisp-tender when pierced with a fork.
- Check the veggies where they touch the pan as these sides often will brown faster than the sides facing up. Stir or turn pieces so that all sides can get brown edges.
- Cook one type of veggie or several types at the same time. If cooking more than one kind of veggie, start with the ones that cook the longest and add those that take less time later.

GENERAL ROASTING TIMES

Here are some basic cooking times for roasting popular veggies. Times will vary based on the size of the veggie pieces and the oven temperature:

Brussels sprouts, carrots, fennel, onions, parsnips, potatoes and sweet potatoes	35 to 45 minutes
Bell peppers, butternut squash, cauliflower and green beans	20 to 25 minutes
Asparagus, eggplant, leeks, pattypan squash and zucchini	15 to 20 minutes

VARIATIONS ▶

ROASTED VEGETABLES (CONTINUED)

Variations

ADDING ROASTED VEGGIES TO OTHER DISHES
Use roasted veggies in omelets or scrambled eggs. Add them to rice or noodle bowls or pizzas, sandwiches and wraps.

BALSAMIC-ROSEMARY ROASTED VEGGIES
Prepare as directed—except line bottom of pan with foil. Add 3 tablespoons balsamic vinegar, 1 tablespoon chopped fresh rosemary leaves and 1 teaspoon Dijon mustard with the oil.

ITALIAN ROASTED VEGGIES
Prepare as directed—except substitute 3 tablespoons Italian dressing for the olive oil, salt, pepper and garlic.

PARMESAN-LEMON ROASTED CAULIFLOWER
Prepare as directed—except increase olive oil to ¼ cup and add ⅛ teaspoon crushed red pepper flakes with the oil. Substitute 7 cups cauliflower florets for the vegetables. Roast 20 to 25 minutes, stirring once, or until cauliflower is tender and golden brown. Toss with ⅔ cup grated Parmesan cheese, 2 tablespoons chopped fresh parsley and 2 teaspoons fresh lemon juice.

SWEET-HOT CUMIN ROASTED VEGGIES
Prepare as directed—except substitute 1 tablespoon honey or maple syrup for 1 tablespoon of the oil. Omit pepper and garlic. Increase salt to 1 teaspoon and add 2 teaspoons ground cumin and 1 teaspoon chili powder with the salt.

GARLICKY GREENS

6 SERVINGS   PREP TIME: **15 MINUTES**   START TO FINISH: **25 MINUTES**

1 **lb kale leaves or beet or collard greens**

1 **tablespoon olive oil**

4 **cloves garlic, chopped**

4 **green onions, thinly sliced**

¼ **cup water**

¼ to ½ **teaspoon crushed red pepper flakes**

2 **teaspoons fresh lemon juice**

½ **teaspoon salt**

1. Remove and discard kale ribs and any tough stems. Wash leaves several times in water, lifting out each time; drain, leaving water on the leaves. Coarsely chop leaves.

2. In 12-inch nonstick skillet, heat oil over medium heat. Add garlic and onion and cook about 1 minute. Add kale, water and pepper flakes; toss. Cover and cook 8 to 10 minutes over low heat, stirring once, or until leaves are tender.

3. Add remaining ingredients and toss lightly.

1 SERVING (½ CUP): CALORIES 70; TOTAL FAT 3G (SATURATED FAT 0G, TRANS FAT 0G); CHOLESTEROL 0MG; SODIUM 230MG; TOTAL CARBOHYDRATE 8G (DIETARY FIBER 3G); PROTEIN 3G **EXCHANGES:** 2 VEGETABLE, ½ FAT **CARBOHYDRATE CHOICES:** ½

Cook your greens to your liking! When cooked less, they will be crisp-tender. If cooked more, they will soften and be easier to chew.

SELECTING AND HANDLING GREENS

- Choose the freshest greens possible—there should be no bruising, discoloration or wilting.
- Keep greens chilled. Store them unwashed in the refrigerator wrapped in a paper towel and placed in a resealable food-storage plastic bag or tightly covered container up to 5 days.
- Wash greens just before using. Rinse well in cold water, removing any dirt. Several types of greens can hold sand and dirt (such as kale, collard and mustard greens), so wash them in several changes of cold water until no dirt remains at the bottom of the bowl.
- Robust greens, such as kale, collard and beet greens, can taste bitter when cooked. To reduce or eliminate the bitterness, add a little salt or acid such as lemon juice.
- Thick stems, ribs and roots can be too tough to eat, so remove as necessary and discard. Serve small leaves whole, but cut up or tear larger leaves into pieces.

Dry greens well—use a salad spinner to quickly and easily remove water from leaves.

Or leaves can be patted dry with kitchen or paper towels.

COOKING GREENS (CHICORY, COLLARDS, ESCAROLE, KALE, MUSTARD, SPINACH, SWISS CHARD AND TURNIP)

For a pound of greens:

See above for Selecting and Handling Greens.

TO STEAM: In saucepan or skillet, place steamer basket in ½ inch of water (water should not touch bottom of basket). Place greens in basket. Cover and heat to boiling; reduce heat to low. Steam 5 to 8 minutes or until tender.

TO MICROWAVE: Place greens in microwavable dish with 2 tablespoons water. Cover and microwave on High for time indicated below:

Beet, chicory and escarole	8 to 10 minutes or until tender
Collards, kale, mustard, spinach, Swiss chard and turnip greens	4 to 6 minutes or until tender

VARIATIONS ▶

Variations

CREAMED GARLICKY GREENS
Prepare as directed—except while greens are cooking, melt ¼ cup butter in 2-quart saucepan over medium heat. Cook 1 chopped small onion in butter until tender, about 5 minutes. Whisk in 3 tablespoons all-purpose flour until smooth and bubbly, stirring constantly, about 3 minutes. Gradually stir in 2½ cups milk, ½ teaspoon salt and ¼ teaspoon pepper. Cook and stir until mixture boils and thickens. Stir cooked greens into milk mixture; serve immediately.

CRUMB-TOPPED GREENS
Prepare as directed—except in small skillet, melt 1 tablespoon butter over medium heat. Stir in ⅓ cup dry bread crumbs. Cook and stir until golden brown. Remove from heat; let cool while preparing greens. Serve crumbs over cooked greens.

GARLICKY PARMESAN GREENS
Prepare as directed—except immediately after cooking, sprinkle greens with ¼ cup grated Parmesan cheese.

SPICY COLLARD AND BEET GREENS
Prepare as directed—except substitute ½ pound collard greens and ½ pound beet greens for the kale. Omit crushed red pepper flakes. Toss 1 tablespoon Sriracha sauce with fresh lemon juice and salt.

SWEET-AND-SOUR SPINACH AND PEPPERS
Prepare as directed—except omit oil. In skillet, cook 2 slices bacon, chopped, until crisp; remove with slotted spoon to paper towel. In bacon drippings in pan cook ½ cup chopped red or yellow bell pepper with garlic and onion over medium heat until softened, about 3 minutes. Omit water. Stir in 1 tablespoon cider vinegar, 2 teaspoons sugar and the crushed red pepper flakes. Add 1 pound spinach, coarsely chopped. Cook just until leaves are wilted. Omit salt.

Build a
DELICIOUS SALAD

Never have a boring salad again! Add an item or two from several or all categories for a different, sensational salad every time.

START WITH THE GREENS
Choose lettuce and/or other greens such as spinach, baby kale or arugula, either individually or in a combination of two or more.

ADD PROTEIN
Bulk up with protein foods such as cooked chicken or salmon, tuna, black or other canned beans, chopped hard-cooked eggs, cheese or tofu. Not only do they add texture, color and interest to your salads, but they help to keep you full longer.

COLOR AND CRUNCH IT UP
Wake up a salad with crunchy, colorful ingredients such as bite-size pieces of raw vegetables, edamame, nuts or seeds such as pomegranate.

SWEETEN THE POT
Toss in small pieces of fresh apple or pear, dried fruit or fresh berries for an irresistible combo.

DRESSED TO KILL
Drizzle with a delicious dressing to tie the ingredients together and add a hit of flavor. Try fresh lemon juice or lime juice or vinegar with olive or vegetable oil, or choose a vinaigrette or creamy salad dressing (see page 173 for flavorful options).

#36

Sweet-and-Sour
COLESLAW

8 SERVINGS   PREP TIME: **15 MINUTES**   START TO FINISH: **3 HOURS 15 MINUTES**

SLAW

- ½ **medium head green cabbage, finely shredded (4 cups)**
- 1 **large carrot, finely shredded (1 cup)**
- 1 **medium green bell pepper, chopped (1 cup)**
- 4 **medium green onions, thinly sliced (¼ cup)**

SWEET-AND-SOUR DRESSING

- ½ **cup sugar**
- ½ **cup white wine vinegar, white vinegar or cider vinegar**
- ¼ **cup vegetable oil**
- 1 **teaspoon ground mustard**
- ½ **teaspoon celery seed**
- ½ **teaspoon salt**

1. In large glass or plastic bowl, toss cabbage, carrot, bell pepper and onions.

2. In tightly covered container, shake dressing ingredients. Pour over vegetables; toss until evenly coated.

3. Cover and refrigerate at least 3 hours, stirring several times, to blend flavors and chill. Stir before serving; serve with slotted spoon.

1 SERVING: CALORIES 140; TOTAL FAT 7G (SATURATED FAT 1G, TRANS FAT 0G); CHOLESTEROL 0MG; SODIUM 170MG; TOTAL CARBOHYDRATE 17G (DIETARY FIBER 1G); PROTEIN 1G **EXCHANGES:** 1 OTHER CARBOHYDRATE, 1 VEGETABLE, 1½ FAT **CARBOHYDRATE CHOICES:** 1

Techniques

CHOOSING CABBAGE

- Choose heads with fresh, firmly packed, crisp leaves. Refrigerate tightly wrapped for up to 1 week.
- Red cabbage is a fun and colorful alternative to green cabbage, or mix and match the varieties for an eye-catching salad.
- Red cabbage will leach its red color when cut, so unless you are comfortable with pink dressing, it's best to use red cabbage with an oil-and-vinegar dressing or use a small amount of red cabbage with mostly green cabbage when using a mayonnaise dressing.

CUTTING CABBAGE

To use a head of cabbage, remove any damaged outer leaves. Cut around the core in a deep cone shape; remove core.

Cut cabbage into fourths. Place one piece, flat side down, on cutting board. Cut into thin slices with large sharp knife. Cut slices several times to make smaller pieces.

CREAMY OR VINAIGRETTE?

Coleslaw lovers often fall into two camps: those who love a vinaigrette-type dressing on their coleslaw and those who like a creamy, mayonnaise-type dressing instead. If you like a vinaigrette-style dressing, use the main recipe. If you like a mayonnaise-type dressing, refer to the recipe variations (page 168). Simply swap out the creamy dressing for the vinaigrette dressing.

MAKE IT A SLAW

Cabbage is only the start when it comes to slaw. You can add other vegetables with the cabbage, or cut up other fruits or veggies into thin, matchstick-like pieces. Tossed with a dressing, slaw can be customized in so many ways! Here are some options:

SLAW SUGGESTIONS

Add these to cabbage, or mix-and-match for alternative slaw recipes:

- Asian pears
- Bell peppers
- Bok choy
- Broccoli stems (or purchase pre-cut broccoli slaw)
- Brussels sprouts (cut crosswise into thin slices)
- Carrots
- Cauliflower stems
- Chiles, fresh
- Cucumbers
- Jicama
- Mango
- Onions
- Radishes

OTHER ADDITIONS

Try adding these less common, but delicious, ingredients to your slaw for a treat:

- Apple, chopped
- Bacon, cooked and crumbled
- Blueberries
- Fruit, dried, such as sweetened cranberries, dried apricots or raisins
- Mandarin orange segments
- Mini marshmallows
- Nuts
- Pineapple tidbits
- Poppy seed
- Strawberries, chopped
- Sesame seed

VARIATIONS ▶

Variations

APPLE-RAISIN COLESLAW

Prepare as directed—except substitute 1 apple cut into thin, matchstick-like, bite-size pieces and 1 cup raisins for the carrot, bell pepper and green onions.

BROCCOLI-CITRUS SLAW

Prepare as directed—except omit cabbage, carrot, bell pepper and Sweet-and-Sour Dressing. Grate 1½ teaspoons zest from 2 clementines; reserve. Add 6 cups broccoli slaw (from two 12-ounce bags) and 2 peeled clementines, separated into segments, with the green onions. In the container, mix 3 tablespoons vegetable oil, 3 tablespoons fresh lemon juice, 4 teaspoons sugar, the reserved clementine zest and ⅛ teaspoon salt. Continue as directed in step 2.

CREAMY COLESLAW

Prepare as directed—except before adding slaw ingredients, in large bowl, mix ½ cup mayonnaise or salad dressing, ¼ cup sour cream, 1 tablespoon sugar, 2 teaspoons each fresh lemon juice and Dijon mustard, ½ teaspoon celery seed (if desired) and ¼ teaspoon each salt and pepper. Toss until evenly coated. Omit Sweet-and-Sour Dressing. Continue as directed in step 2.

EASY ASIAN SLAW

Prepare as directed—except omit bell pepper and Sweet-and-Sour Dressing. Add ⅓ cup chopped fresh cilantro and 1 package (3 ounces) oriental-flavor ramen noodle soup mix with the cabbage, breaking up the noodles into small pieces and reserving the seasoning packet for another use. Toss with ⅔ cup Asian sesame and ginger dressing and ½ cup chopped peanuts.

SOUTHWEST SLAW

Prepare as directed—except omit carrot and Sweet-and-Sour Dressing. Add 1 can (11 ounces) drained whole kernel corn with bell peppers with the cabbage. In the container, shake 1½ tablespoons sugar, 4½ tablespoons cider vinegar, 1½ tablespoons vegetable oil, ¾ teaspoon pepper and ½ teaspoon salt. Continue as directed in step 2.

#37

~Fresh Herb~
VINAIGRETTE

12 SERVINGS PREP TIME: **10 MINUTES** START TO FINISH: **10 MINUTES**

½ cup extra-virgin olive oil

¼ cup white wine vinegar

2 tablespoons minced shallot or onion

1 tablespoon chopped fresh basil, thyme or oregano or a combination of favorite herbs

1 teaspoon sugar

1 teaspoon Dijon mustard

½ teaspoon salt

¼ teaspoon freshly ground black pepper

1. In blender container or bowl of food processor, place all ingredients. Blend on high speed 15 to 20 seconds or until well blended. Alternatively, place all ingredients in container with tightly fitting lid. Shake vigorously until well blended.

2. Cover and refrigerate until ready to use. If ingredients have separated, whisk until blended.

1 TABLESPOON: CALORIES 80; TOTAL FAT 9G (SATURATED FAT 1G, TRANS FAT 0G); CHOLESTEROL 0MG; SODIUM 110MG; TOTAL CARBOHYDRATE 0G (DIETARY FIBER 0G); PROTEIN 0G **EXCHANGES:** 2 FAT **CARBOHYDRATE CHOICES:** 0

TEST KITCHEN TIP

Prepare your vinaigrette ahead of time to allow the flavors to blend. No time to make it ahead? Make it first when preparing your meal! Cover and refrigerate it while you get everything else on the table.

Techniques

See Salad Dressing Basics (page 175).
See What Is an Emulsion? (page 175).

WORKING WITH HERBS

Fresh herbs are less potent than dried herbs. In general, use one-third less dried herbs than fresh. So,1 tablespoon chopped fresh basil leaves is equal to 1 teaspoon dried leaves.

CHOOSING HERB COMBINATIONS

- Mix and match what herbs you have on hand, find on sale or are fresh at the farmer's market for a different dressing every time!
- Use strong herbs sparingly so as not to overpower other milder herbs or make the dressing too strong in flavor.
- Some herbs work well together. Consider adding a blending herb when using a combination of two or three herbs in your dressings.

STRONG HERBS (USE SPARINGLY)

- Horseradish root
- Mint
- Oregano
- Rosemary
- Thyme

BLENDING HERBS

- Curly parsley
- Italian (flat-leaf) parsley
- Savory

OTHER USES FOR VINAIGRETTE

- Toss vinaigrette with roasted or grilled vegetables.
- Toss with hot, cooked pasta.
- Use as a dipping sauce for crusty bread.
- Drizzle over grilled chicken or fish.

VARIATIONS ▶

FRESH HERB VINAIGRETTE (CONTINUED)

Variations

LEMON-LAVENDER VINAIGRETTE
Prepare as directed—except substitute fresh lemon juice for the vinegar, 2 to 3 teaspoons chopped fresh lavender or mint for the herbs and 2 tablespoons honey for the sugar. Serve with fruit or in salads containing fruit.

ORANGE-HERB VINAIGRETTE
Prepare as directed—except decrease vinegar to 1 tablespoon. Add ¼ cup fresh orange juice and ⅛ teaspoon hot pepper sauce.

RED WINE–HERB VINAIGRETTE
Prepare as directed—except substitute red wine vinegar for the white wine vinegar. Increase sugar to 2 teaspoons.

SOUTHWESTERN VINAIGRETTE
Prepare as directed—except add 2 teaspoons taco seasoning mix (from 1-ounce package) with the sugar.

SUN-DRIED TOMATO VINAIGRETTE
Prepare as directed—except omit herbs. Add ¼ cup chopped sun-dried tomatoes packed in olive oil and herbs with the shallot.

#38

Creamy
BALSAMIC DRESSING

16 SERVINGS   PREP TIME: **10 MINUTES**   START TO FINISH: **10 MINUTES**

¼ **cup balsamic vinegar**

3 **tablespoons honey**

2 **tablespoons chopped fresh basil**

1 **tablespoon fresh lemon juice**

1 **tablespoon Dijon mustard**

1¼ **teaspoons salt**

⅛ **teaspoon freshly ground pepper**

1 **clove garlic, finely chopped**

¾ **cup extra-virgin olive oil**

In blender or food processor, place all ingredients except oil. Blend on high speed 30 to 40 seconds or until smooth. Slowly drizzle in oil through feed tube and continue blending until thick and creamy.

1 TABLESPOON: CALORIES 110; TOTAL FAT 10G (SATURATED FAT 1.5G, TRANS FAT 0G); CHOLESTEROL 0MG; SODIUM 60MG; TOTAL CARBOHYDRATE 4G (DIETARY FIBER 0G); PROTEIN 0G **EXCHANGES:** ½ OTHER CARBOHYDRATE, 2 FAT **CARBOHYDRATE CHOICES:** 0

TEST KITCHEN TIP

You can use red or white balsamic vinegar. The red variety will give the dressing (and other foods it's used with) a reddish-brown appearance. The white variety won't add color to your dressings or other foods you use it on. White balsamic vinegar tends to be more mild in flavor than red.

SALAD DRESSING BASICS

- The base for most salad dressings is some type of oil plus vinegar, or another acidic ingredient, typically in a ratio of 3 parts oil to 1 part vinegar.
- Oil provides the body and may add flavor to the dressing, depending on the type used, or may simply carry the flavor of the other ingredients.
- Depending on the oil and vinegar used, you can change the flavor of your vinaigrette every time you make it. Try one of these alternative oils or vinegars:

OILS: Almond, avocado, sesame or walnut

VINEGARS: Cider, fruit, herb, rice, white or wine (champagne, sherry, red or white)

ALTERNATIVES TO VINEGAR

Another way to change the flavor of your dressing is to use another acidic ingredient in place of the vinegar. Try citrus juice (grapefruit, lemon, lime or orange) or red or white wine, sherry or champagne.

WHAT IS AN EMULSION?

Most salad dressings make an emulsion—a method and mixture of ingredients that keeps the ingredients mixed, at least long enough to enjoy.

- Simple vinaigrette ingredients will separate over time, so if you store your dressings in the refrigerator, you probably will find the ingredients have separated out after storage. Simply recombine them using a whisk, hand blender, blender or food processor when ready to use.
- Creamy-style salad dressings are permanent emulsions—they have an added ingredient that keeps the ingredients combined (an emulsifier). Mayonnaise, for example, is a permanent emulsion.
- Mayonnaise or egg yolks are the typical ingredients used as emulsifiers in creamy salad dressings. If using egg yolks, use pasteurized eggs because regular raw eggs may contain salmonella if not cooked. Ingesting even the smallest amount of salmonella can cause sickness.

VARIATIONS ▶

Variations

BEET SALAD
Place 5 cups (4 ounces) baby arugula on serving plate. Top with cooked sliced beets, crumbled goat cheese and chopped toasted pecans. Drizzle with ¼ cup Creamy Balsamic Dressing.

FRESH BERRY SALAD WITH CREAMY BALSAMIC DRESSING
Place 6 cups (5 ounces) kale and arugula blend on serving plate. Top with quartered strawberries, fresh raspberries, fresh blackberries, toasted slivered almonds and crumbled feta cheese. Drizzle with ¼ cup Creamy Balsamic Dressing (see page 174).

HERBED BALSAMIC DRESSING
Prepare as directed—except add 1 to 2 tablespoons chopped fresh chives with the basil leaves.

JALAPEÑO BALSAMIC DRESSING
Prepare as directed—except add 1 seeded and chopped medium jalapeño chile with the basil.

RASPBERRY-ALMOND VINAIGRETTE
Prepare as directed—except substitute almond oil for the olive oil and raspberry vinegar for the balsamic vinegar.

Breads
TO DEVOUR

Blueberry MUFFINS

12 MUFFINS   PREP TIME: **10 MINUTES**   START TO FINISH: **40 MINUTES**

¾ **cup milk**

¼ **cup vegetable oil or melted butter**

1 **egg**

2 **cups all-purpose flour**

½ **cup granulated sugar**

2 **teaspoons baking powder**

½ **teaspoon salt**

1 **cup fresh, canned (drained) or frozen (do not thaw) blueberries**

2 **tablespoons coarse sugar or additional granulated sugar, if desired**

1. Heat oven to 400°F. Grease bottoms only of 12 regular-size muffin cups with shortening or cooking spray, or place paper baking cup in each muffin cup.

2. In large bowl, beat milk, oil and egg with fork or whisk until well mixed. Stir in flour, granulated sugar, baking powder and salt all at once just until flour is moistened. Fold in blueberries. Divide batter evenly among muffin cups; sprinkle each with ½ teaspoon coarse sugar.

3. Bake 20 to 25 minutes or until golden brown and toothpick inserted in center comes out clean. If baked in greased pan, let stand about 5 minutes in pan, then remove from pan to cooling rack; if baked in paper baking cups, immediately remove from pan to cooling rack. Serve warm if desired.

1 MUFFIN: CALORIES 170; TOTAL FAT 6G (SATURATED FAT 1G, TRANS FAT 0G); CHOLESTEROL 20MG; SODIUM 190MG; TOTAL CARBOHYDRATE 27G (DIETARY FIBER 0G); PROTEIN 3G **EXCHANGES**: 1 STARCH, 1 FRUIT, 1 FAT **CARBOHYDRATE CHOICES:** 2

Techniques

MAKING BEAUTIFUL MUFFINS

Stir in dry ingredients all at once, just until flour is moistened. Fold in blueberries.

Divide batter evenly among muffin cups using spring-handled scoop or two spoons.

USING THE RIGHT PAN

- For golden-brown color and tender crusts, use shiny pans to reflect the heat. If using dark or nonstick pans, reduce oven temperature by 25°F. They absorb heat more easily than shiny pans, causing baked goods to brown too quickly.
- Grease bottoms only of muffin cups unless otherwise specified. This prevents a lip and a hard, dry edge from forming.
- Allow at least 2 inches of space around pans in the oven for heat circulation.

TIPS FOR GREAT MUFFINS

- See Measuring Ingredients (page 195).
- Mix muffin batter with a spoon (not a mixer) just until the dry ingredients are moistened (the batter will be lumpy) to avoid muffins that are tough with peaked tops.
- To prevent muffins from getting soggy or gummy, don't use more fruit than called for in the recipe. Be sure fresh berries are well drained after washing or use frozen berries (do not thaw).
- Remove the muffins from the pan as directed. Cool on cooling rack so that they won't get soft and lose their shape from the steam, which happens if they are left in pans to cool.
- For perfectly baked muffins, set your timer for the minimum time stated in the recipe. When the timer goes off, check for doneness using the doneness indicator(s) stated in the recipe. If the doneness indicators haven't happened, bake a minute or two longer and check again.

VARIATIONS ▶

Variations

APPLE-CINNAMON MUFFINS
Prepare as directed—except omit blueberries. Stir in 1 cup chopped peeled apple (1 medium) and ½ teaspoon ground cinnamon with the flour. Bake 25 to 30 minutes.

BANANA MUFFINS
Prepare as directed—except omit blueberries. Reduce milk to ⅓ cup. Beat in 1 cup mashed very ripe bananas (2 medium) with the milk. Substitute packed brown sugar for the granulated sugar.

CHOCOLATE CHIP MUFFINS
Prepare as directed—except substitute 1 cup miniature semisweet chocolate chips for the blueberries.

LEMON-POPPY SEED MUFFINS
Omit blueberries and coarse sugar. Prepare as directed—except increase milk to 1 cup. Stir ¼ cup grated lemon zest in with the milk. Stir 2 tablespoons fresh lemon juice into egg mixture. Add 2 teaspoons poppy seed with the baking powder. Mix ½ cup powdered sugar and 2 to 3 teaspoons fresh lemon juice (½ teaspoon at a time) until smooth and drizzling consistency. Drizzle over warm muffins.

SNICKERDOODLE MUFFINS
Prepare as directed—except add ½ teaspoon ground cinnamon with the flour. Omit blueberries and coarse sugar. In shallow bowl, mix 1 tablespoon granulated sugar and 1 teaspoon ground cinnamon. Dip and swirl warm muffin tops in cinnamon-sugar.

STREUSEL-TOPPED BLUEBERRY MUFFINS
Prepare as directed—except omit coarse sugar. In medium bowl, mix ¼ cup all-purpose flour, ¼ cup packed brown sugar and ¼ teaspoon ground cinnamon. Cut in 2 tablespoons cold butter, using pastry blender or fork, until crumbly. Sprinkle 1 tablespoon streusel over batter in each muffin cup.

BANANA BREAD

2 LOAVES (12 SLICES EACH)   PREP TIME: **15 MINUTES**
START TO FINISH: **3 HOURS 40 MINUTES**

1¼ cups sugar

½ cup butter, softened

2 eggs

1½ cups mashed very ripe bananas (3 medium)

½ cup buttermilk

1 teaspoon vanilla

2½ cups all-purpose flour

1 teaspoon baking soda

1 teaspoon salt

1 cup chopped nuts, if desired

1. Heat oven to 350°F. Grease bottoms only of 2 (8x4- or 9x5-inch) loaf pans with shortening or cooking spray.

2. In large bowl, stir sugar and butter until well mixed. Stir in eggs until well mixed. Stir in bananas, buttermilk and vanilla; beat with spoon until smooth. Stir in flour, baking soda and salt just until moistened. Stir in nuts. Divide batter evenly between pans.

3. Bake 8-inch loaves about 1 hour and 9-inch loaves about 1 hour 15 minutes, or until toothpick inserted in center comes out clean. Cool 10 minutes in pans on cooling rack.

4. Loosen sides of loaves from pans; remove from pans and place top side up on cooling rack. Cool completely, about 2 hours, before slicing. Wrap tightly and store at room temperature up to 4 days, or refrigerate up to 1 week.

1 SLICE: CALORIES 150; TOTAL FAT 4.5G (SATURATED FAT 2.5G, TRANS FAT 0G); CHOLESTEROL 30MG; SODIUM 190MG; TOTAL CARBOHYDRATE 24G (DIETARY FIBER 0G); PROTEIN 2G **EXCHANGES:** ½ STARCH, 1 OTHER CARBOHYDRATE, 1 FAT **CARBOHYDRATE CHOICES:** 1½

Techniques

MAKING GREAT QUICK BREADS

See Using the Right Pan (page 181).

See Measuring Ingredients (page 195).

See Tips for Great Muffins (page 181)—they work for other quick breads, such as Banana Bread, too.

CUTTING QUICK BREADS

- Cool loaves completely, about 2 hours, to prevent crumbling when sliced.
- Cut loaves with a serrated knife using a light sawing motion.
- Slicing is easier if loaves have been refrigerated 24 hours.

STORING QUICK BREADS

The flavor improves if loaves have been refrigerated 24 hours.

To store, wrap completely cooled loaves tightly in plastic wrap or foil and refrigerate up to 1 week.

To freeze, place tightly wrapped loaves in freezer plastic bags and freeze up to 3 months.

VARIATIONS ▶

BANANA BREAD (CONTINUED)

Variations

APRICOT-BANANA BREAD
Prepare as directed—except stir 1 cup chopped dried apricots in with the nuts. Use chopped pecans for the nuts.

BANANA–CHOCOLATE CHIP BREAD
Prepare as directed—except substitute semisweet or milk chocolate chips for the nuts.

BLUEBERRY-BANANA BREAD
Prepare as directed—except substitute 1 cup fresh or frozen (do not thaw) blueberries for the nuts.

CRANBERRY-ORANGE BANANA BREAD
Prepare as directed—except add ¼ cup grated orange zest (from 2 large oranges) with the bananas. Substitute ½ cup dried sweetened cranberries for ½ cup of the nuts. When loaves are cool, in small bowl, mix 1 cup powdered sugar and enough fresh orange juice (4 to 6 tablespoons) until smooth and drizzling consistency. Drizzle over loaves. Let icing set before wrapping and storing.

STRAWBERRY-BANANA BREAD
Prepare as directed—except substitute 1 cup chopped fresh strawberries for the nuts.

POPOVERS

6 POPOVERS   PREP TIME: **10 MINUTES**   START TO FINISH: **45 MINUTES**

2   eggs
1   cup all-purpose flour
1   cup milk
½   teaspoon salt

1. Heat oven to 450°F. Generously grease 6-cup popover pan or large muffin pan with shortening. Heat pan in oven 5 minutes.

2. Meanwhile, in medium bowl, beat eggs slightly with fork or whisk. Beat in remaining ingredients just until smooth (do not overbeat or popovers may not puff as high). Divide batter evenly among popover cups, filling each about half full.

3. Bake 20 minutes. Reduce oven temperature to 325°F. Bake 10 to 15 minutes longer or until deep golden brown. Immediately remove from pan. Serve hot.

1 POPOVER: CALORIES 120; TOTAL FAT 3G (SATURATED FAT 1G, TRANS FAT 0G); CHOLESTEROL 75MG; SODIUM 240MG; TOTAL CARBOHYDRATE 18G (DIETARY FIBER 0G); PROTEIN 6G **EXCHANGES:** 1 STARCH, 1 FAT **CARBOHYDRATE CHOICES:** 1

Make a delicious spread for your popovers by stirring in 2 tablespoons honey or maple syrup into ½ cup softened butter with a whisk.

Techniques

POPOVER SUCCESS

See Measuring Ingredients (page 195).

- Greasing the pan generously helps in removing the popovers from the pan without any areas sticking. Any parts of the popovers that stick to the pan could cause them to deflate when removed.
- Heating the pan 5 minutes before adding the batter and baking at a high temperature creates steam quickly, causing the popovers to rise nice and high.
- Beat in the flour, milk and salt just until smooth. If overbeaten, the popovers may not rise as high.
- Reduce the heat to set the popovers without overbaking them.
- Immediately and carefully remove the popovers from the pan. Serve immediately to prevent them from collapsing.
- Help prevent the popovers from collapsing by immediately after removing them from the pan, pierce the tops in a few places with the point of a sharp paring knife to allow the steam to escape.

MAKE-AHEAD POPOVERS

Immediately after baking, pierce baked popovers as described above. Cool completely on cooling rack. To reheat, place popovers on an ungreased cookie sheet; bake at 350°F 5 minutes.

Variations

CHEDDAR-DILL POPOVERS

Prepare as directed—except add ¼ cup shredded Cheddar cheese and ½ teaspoon dried dill weed with the milk.

GARLICKY POPOVERS

Prepare as directed—except add 1 finely chopped clove garlic with the milk.

LEMON-CHIVE POPOVERS

Prepare as directed—except add 2 teaspoons chopped fresh chives and 1 teaspoon grated lemon zest with the milk.

YORKSHIRE PUDDING

Heat oven to 350°F. Place ¼ cup vegetable oil or meat drippings in 9-inch square pan; place pan in oven and heat until hot. Increase oven temperature to 450°F. Prepare popover batter as directed in step 2; carefully pour batter into hot oil. Bake 18 to 23 minutes or until puffy and golden brown (pudding will puff during baking but will deflate shortly after removal from oven). Cut into squares; serve immediately.

BASIL–GARLIC BUTTER FOR POPOVERS

In small bowl, mix ½ cup softened butter with 2 tablespoons chopped fresh basil leaves, 1 tablespoon finely chopped red onion and 1 chopped clove garlic. Let stand at room temperature while preparing Popovers. To make ahead, cover and refrigerate up to 2 weeks in advance. Let stand at room temperature about 30 minutes to soften before using.

CUSTOMIZABLE MUFFINS

Muffin Base + Stir-In + Topping = Customizable Muffins anytime!

MUFFIN BASE

12 MUFFINS   PREP TIME: **10 MINUTES**   TOTAL: **40 MINUTES**

¾ **cup milk**

¼ **cup vegetable oil or melted butter**

1 **egg**

2 **cups all-purpose flour**

½ **cup granulated sugar**

2 **teaspoons baking powder**

½ **teaspoon salt**

Desired Stir-In (see options below)

Desired Topping (see options opposite)

1. Heat oven to 400°F. Grease bottoms only of 12 regular-size muffin cups with shortening or cooking spray, or place paper baking cup in each muffin cup.

2. In large bowl, beat milk, oil and egg with fork or whisk until well mixed. Stir in flour, granulated sugar, baking powder and salt all at once just until flour is moistened (batter will be lumpy). Fold in desired stir-in. Divide batter evenly among muffin cups; sprinkle with desired topping.

3. Bake 20 to 25 minutes or until golden brown and toothpick inserted in center comes out clean. If baked in greased pan, let stand about 5 minutes in pan, then remove from pan to cooling rack; if baked in paper baking cups, immediately remove from pan to cooling rack. Serve warm if desired.

STIR-INS

Choose one of these stir-ins to add to the muffin base in the amount called for. You can add two ingredients together, just be sure to use half the amount called for of each ingredient.

Apple —1 cup chopped fresh apple + 1 teaspoon ground cinnamon

Apricot —1 cup chopped dried apricots

Banana —1 cup mashed ripe banana (decrease milk to ⅓ cup, substitute brown sugar for the granulated sugar)

Blueberry —1 cup fresh or frozen (do not thaw) blueberries

Carrot —¾ cup finely shredded carrot + 1 teaspoon ground cinnamon

Cherry —1 cup dried tart cherries or 1 jar (10 ounces) drained chopped maraschino cherries

Chocolate Chip—1 cup semisweet, milk or dark chocolate chips

Corn —¾ cup whole kernel fresh corn + 2 tablespoons chopped fresh basil leaves

Date —1 cup chopped pitted dates

Nut —1 cup chopped peanuts, pecans or walnuts

Peach —1 cup chopped fresh or frozen (do not thaw) peaches or drained canned peaches

Pear —1 cup chopped fresh ripe pear + ½ teaspoon ground cinnamon + ¼ teaspoon ground nutmeg

Raisin —1 cup raisins

Raspberries —1 cup fresh or frozen (do not thaw) raspberries

Zucchini — ¾ cup finely shredded zucchini + 1 teaspoon ground cinnamon

TOPPINGS

Sprinkle muffin batter in pan with one of the following ingredients before baking.

Almond —¼ cup sliced almonds

Coarse Sugar —2 tablespoons coarse sugar

Cinnamon-Sugar —1 tablespoon sugar + ¼ teaspoon ground cinnamon

Citrus-Sugar —1 tablespoon sugar + 1 teaspoon grated orange or lemon peel or a combination

Spiced Oat —1 tablespoon old-fashioned or quick-cooking oats + 1 tablespoon sugar + ¼ teaspoon ground cinnamon

Streusel —¼ cup all-purpose flour + ¼ cup packed brown sugar + ¼ teaspoon ground cinnamon; cut in 2 tablespoons cold butter with fork until crumbly

1 Raspberry with Citrus-Sugar
2 Apricot Almond
3 Zucchini-Streusel
4 Blueberry with Spiced Oat
5 Carrot with Cinnamon-Sugar
6 Chocolate Chip

PANCAKES

9 (4-INCH) PANCAKES   PREP TIME: **25 MINUTES**   START TO FINISH: **25 MINUTES**

1   **egg**

1   **cup all-purpose or whole wheat flour**

¾   **cup milk**

2   **tablespoons vegetable oil or melted butter**

1   **tablespoon sugar**

3   **teaspoons baking powder**

¼   **teaspoon salt**

1. In medium bowl, beat egg with whisk until fluffy. Stir in remaining ingredients just until flour is moistened.

2. Heat griddle or skillet over medium-high heat (375°F).

3. For each pancake, pour slightly less than ¼ cup batter onto hot griddle. Cook 2 to 3 minutes or until bubbly on top and dry around edges. Turn; cook other side until golden brown.

1 PANCAKE: CALORIES 110; TOTAL FAT 5G (SATURATED FAT 1.5G, TRANS FAT 0G); CHOLESTEROL 25MG; SODIUM 250MG; TOTAL CARBOHYDRATE 13G (DIETARY FIBER 0G); PROTEIN 3G **EXCHANGES:** 1 STARCH, ½ FAT **CARBOHYDRATE CHOICES:** 1

TEST KITCHEN TIP

Mix the pancake batter in a bowl with a pouring spout, a 4-cup liquid measuring cup or pitcher to easily pour the batter onto the pan. Measure the batter for the first pancake to see the size it is supposed to be before pouring the remaining batter on the griddle. (See Cook a Test Pancake, right.)

MAKING GREAT PANCAKES

The key to making the perfect pancakes is properly measuring the ingredients.

MEASURING INGREDIENTS

- Measure the flour by spooning it into a dry measuring cup and leveling it off with the straight edge of a knife or metal spatula.
- Use a liquid measuring cup for the milk, placing it on the counter to fill it and reading the amount by checking it at eye level.
- If using butter, use real butter to ensure the pancakes have the best taste and texture.
- Check the expiration date of your baking powder for freshness. Old baking powder may prevent the pancakes from rising properly.

MIXING AND COOKING TIPS

- Whisk the ingredients just until the flour is moistened. The batter will be slightly lumpy. Overmixing can make the pancakes turn out tough.
- Brush the griddle or skillet with vegetable oil or spray with cooking spray before heating.
- To test if the pan is hot enough, wet your fingers with just a small amount of water. Shake your fingers over the pan so that a few drops of water fall onto the pan. If the bubbles jump around and sizzle, the pan is hot enough.
- Cook a test pancake to see how you like the thickness. Some people like pancakes thicker or thinner than the average thickness.
- Adjust the batter, adding 1 to 2 tablespoons additional flour if thicker pancakes are desired, or 1 to 2 tablespoons additional milk if thinner pancakes are desired.
- To keep pancakes hot until all of them are cooked, place a cooling rack on top of a cookie sheet in a 200°F oven. Place each pancake on the cooling rack as it is cooked; cover loosely with foil. The cooling rack allows the steam to escape from the hot pancakes to maintain their texture as well as their heat while you're cooking the remaining pancakes.

VARIATIONS ▶

Variations

BERRY PANCAKES
Prepare as directed—except stir ½ cup fresh or frozen (thawed and well drained) blackberries, blueberries or raspberries into batter.

BUTTERMILK PANCAKES
Prepare as directed—except substitute 1 cup buttermilk for the milk. Reduce baking powder to 1 teaspoon. Add ½ teaspoon baking soda.

CHURRO PANCAKES WITH CHOCOLATE GLAZE
Prepare as directed—except before making pancakes, heat ⅓ cup chocolate chips and ¼ cup heavy whipping cream in small microwavable bowl on High about 30 seconds or until mixture can be stirred smooth. Gradually stir in ½ cup powdered sugar. Sprinkle each serving with cinnamon-sugar and drizzle with the chocolate glaze.

PANCAKES WITH FRUITY YOGURT TOPPING
Prepare as directed—except mix 2 containers (6 ounces each) French vanilla yogurt with ½ cup strawberry or other flavor fruit preserves. Serve pancakes with yogurt topping instead of syrup.

WHOLE-GRAIN STRAWBERRY PANCAKES
Prepare as directed—except substitute whole-grain flour for the all-purpose flour. Top each serving with ¼ cup strawberry yogurt and ½ cup sliced fresh strawberries.

#43

~Raised
BELGIAN WAFFLES

8 (7½-INCH) WAFFLES   PREP TIME: 55 MINUTES   START TO FINISH: 1 HOUR 25 MINUTES

2¾   cups milk
1   **package fast-acting dry yeast (2¼ teaspoons)**
½   **cup sugar**
3   **eggs, separated**
¾   **cup butter, melted**
2   **teaspoons vanilla**
1   **teaspoon salt**
4   **cups all-purpose flour**

TOPPINGS, IF DESIRED
   Blueberry syrup
   Whipped cream
   Fresh blueberries

1. In 1-cup microwavable measuring cup, microwave ¼ cup milk on High 10 to 20 seconds or until it reaches 110°F to 115°F. Stir in yeast and ½ teaspoon sugar. Let stand 5 minutes or until foamy. In 4-cup microwavable measuring cup, heat remaining 2½ cups milk on High 2 to 3 minutes or until it reaches 120°F to 130°F.

2. In large bowl, beat warm milk, remaining sugar, the egg yolks, butter, vanilla and salt with whisk until well blended. Beat in yeast mixture and flour until smooth.

3. In medium bowl, beat egg whites with electric mixer until stiff peaks form. Fold into batter until small flecks of white are visible. Cover; let stand 30 minutes or until batter starts to rise.

4. Spray Belgian waffle maker with cooking spray; heat waffle maker. Gently stir batter; spoon into waffle maker. Close lid. Bake 4 minutes or until steaming stops and waffle is golden brown. Serve with syrup, whipped cream and blueberries.

1 WAFFLE: CALORIES 500; TOTAL FAT 22G (SATURATED FAT 13G, TRANS FAT 1G); CHOLESTEROL 130MG; SODIUM 480MG; TOTAL CARBOHYDRATE 65G (DIETARY FIBER 2G); PROTEIN 12G **EXCHANGES:** 3½ STARCH, 1 OTHER CARBOHYDRATE, 4 FAT **CARBOHYDRATE CHOICES:** 4

Techniques

MAKING LIGHT AND FLUFFY BELGIAN WAFFLES

See Measuring Ingredients (page 195).

- Belgian waffles are made with a special Belgian waffle iron, which has deeper indentations than a regular waffle iron, for thick-yet-light-and-fluffy waffles.
- We make the batter light and fluffy in two ways: raising with yeast as well as folding stiffly beaten egg whites into the batter, adding air to the batter.

WORKING WITH YEAST

- Yeast needs the proper environment in order to grow.
- Fast-acting yeast cuts down on the rise time needed. It needs to be added to liquids at a higher temperature than traditional yeast does.
- Yeast is temperature sensitive. If the milk is too hot, it can kill the yeast. If the milk is too cool, it can prevent growth.
- A little sugar is added with the milk and acts as food for the yeast, encouraging it to grow.
- Use an instant-read thermometer to be sure your milk is the correct temperature.
- Always check the expiration date of yeast before you use it.

MAKE THE BATTER AHEAD

The waffle batter can be made up to 24 hours in advance. Lightly spoon the batter into a container twice its volume (the batter will continue to rise). Cover loosely and refrigerate. Stir the batter down to its original volume before using.

MAKING BEAUTIFUL WAFFLES

If you're purchasing a Belgian waffle maker, the depth of plates can vary. For the most dramatic waffles, look for those with the deepest wells for batter.

For evenly golden-brown waffles, be sure to heat the waffle iron well before adding the batter. If your waffles come out uneven in color, try a technique discovered by our food stylists: Set the doneness dial to high before adding the batter. Once the batter is added, adjust the dial back to a lower setting. Repeat for each waffle.

VARIATIONS ▶

Variations

BELGIAN WAFFLE EGG SANDWICHES

Prepare as directed—except cut waffles in half horizontally. For each sandwich, spread 1 tablespoon mayonnaise on one side of each half. Place lettuce leaves, sliced tomatoes, 1 fried egg, and 1 (1-ounce) slice Cheddar or pepper Jack cheese on top of one waffle half. Cover with other waffle half, mayonnaise side down. Secure sandwich with toothpicks, if desired.

BELGIAN WAFFLES WITH BERRY CREAM

Prepare as directed—except before making waffles, in small chilled bowl, beat ⅔ cup heavy whipping cream and 2 tablespoons powdered sugar with electric mixer on high speed until stiff peaks form. Fold in 1 cup chopped fresh strawberries and ¼ cup fresh blueberries. Refrigerate until ready to serve.

BUTTERMILK-BACON BELGIAN WAFFLES

Prepare as directed—except substitute buttermilk for the milk. Stir 10 slices crisply cooked and crumbled bacon into batter just before cooking waffles.

CHOCOLATE CHIP–ORANGE BELGIAN WAFFLES

Prepare as directed—except stir 1 cup miniature chocolate chips and ¼ cup grated orange zest (from 2 large oranges) into batter before cooking waffles. Make Orange Cream to serve with the waffles: In medium bowl, beat 1½ cups heavy whipping cream and ¼ cup powdered sugar with electric mixer on high speed until soft peaks form. Beat in ¼ cup (thawed) frozen orange juice concentrate. Refrigerate until ready to serve.

WAFFLE ICE-CREAM SANDWICHES

Prepare as directed—except cool completely on cooling rack. Spread any flavor of ice cream between two waffles. Wrap tightly in plastic wrap and freeze. Cut into 4 to 6 wedges.

If desired, dip waffle points into melted chocolate and sprinkle with finely chopped nuts, shredded coconut or sprinkles. Place on cooking parchment paper–lined cookie sheet; freeze until chocolate is firm. If not serving right away, wrap wedges tightly in plastic wrap and store in freezer until ready to serve.

44

Caramel
STICKY ROLLS

15 ROLLS   PREP TIME: **40 MINUTES**   START TO FINISH: **3 HOURS 20 MINUTES**

ROLLS

3½ to 4 **cups all-purpose or bread flour**

⅓ **cup granulated sugar**

1 **teaspoon salt**

2 **packages regular active or fast-acting dry yeast (4½ teaspoons)**

1 **cup very warm milk (120°F to 130°F)**

¼ **cup butter, softened**

1 **egg**

CARAMEL TOPPING

1 **cup packed brown sugar**

½ **cup butter, softened**

¼ **cup light corn syrup**

1 **cup pecan halves, if desired**

FILLING

½ **cup chopped pecans or raisins, if desired**

¼ **cup granulated sugar or packed brown sugar**

1 **teaspoon ground cinnamon**

2 **tablespoons butter, softened**

1. In large bowl, mix 2 cups of the flour, ⅓ cup granulated sugar, the salt and yeast. Add warm milk, ¼ cup butter and the egg. Beat with electric mixer on low speed 1 minute, scraping bowl frequently. Beat on medium speed 1 minute, scraping bowl frequently. Stir in enough of remaining flour, ½ cup at a time, to make dough easy to handle.

2. Place dough on lightly floured surface. Knead about 5 minutes or until dough is smooth and springy. Grease large bowl with shortening. Place dough in bowl, turning dough to grease all sides. Cover bowl loosely with plastic wrap and let rise in warm place about 1 hour 30 minutes or until dough has doubled in size. Dough is ready if indentation remains when dough is touched.

3. In 2-quart saucepan, heat brown sugar and ½ cup butter to boiling, stirring constantly; remove from heat. Stir in corn syrup. Pour into 13x9-inch pan. Sprinkle with pecan halves.

4. In small bowl, mix filling ingredients except 2 tablespoons butter; set aside.

5. Gently push fist into dough to deflate. On lightly floured surface, flatten dough with hands or rolling pin into 15x10-inch rectangle. Spread with the 2 tablespoons butter; sprinkle with filling. Roll rectangle up tightly, beginning at 15-inch side. Pinch edge of dough into roll to seal. With fingers, shape roll until even. With dental floss or serrated knife, cut roll into 15 (1-inch) slices.

6. Place slices slightly apart in pan, cut side down. Cover loosely with plastic wrap and let rise in warm place about 30 minutes or until dough has doubled in size.

7. Heat oven to 350°F. Uncover rolls. Bake 30 to 35 minutes or until golden brown. Let stand 2 to 3 minutes. Place heatproof plate upside down over pan; turn plate and pan over. Let stand 1 minute so caramel can drizzle over rolls; remove pan. Serve warm.

1 ROLL: CALORIES 320; TOTAL FAT 12G (SATURATED FAT 6G, TRANS FAT 0.5G); CHOLESTEROL 45MG; SODIUM 250MG; TOTAL CARBOHYDRATE 50G (DIETARY FIBER 1G); PROTEIN 4G **EXCHANGES:** 1 STARCH, 2½ OTHER CARBOHYDRATE, 2 FAT **CARBOHYDRATE CHOICES:** 3

Techniques

MAKING GREAT CINNAMON ROLLS
See Measuring Ingredients (page 195).
See Working with Yeast (page 199).

KNEADING YEAST DOUGH
- Properly kneading yeast dough helps the dough rise and produces bread or rolls with a finer texture and finer crumb.
- When flour is mixed with liquid, gluten strands are formed. Kneading makes the gluten stronger and more elastic, allowing the dough to stretch and to expand and hold its shape as it rises and bakes.
- Yeast dough recipes usually offer a range of how much flour to use to adjust for the conditions when you are baking. The flour can have more or less moisture in it, depending on the weather (humidity) when baking and the conditions under which it has been stored, which can affect the moisture level of the bread.
- Start with the minimum amount of flour, adding more (a little at a time) as needed while kneading, until the dough becomes smooth and elastic.

MAKE-AHEAD CARAMEL STICKY ROLLS
After placing slices in pan, cover tightly with plastic wrap or foil; refrigerate at least 4 and up to 24 hours. About 2 hours before baking, remove from refrigerator. Remove plastic wrap or foil and cover loosely with plastic wrap. Let rise in warm place until dough has doubled in size. If some rising has occurred in the refrigerator, rising time may be less than 2 hours. Bake as directed.

VARIATIONS ▶

Variations

CHOCOLATE-CARAMEL STICKY ROLLS
Prepare as directed—except add ½ cup baking cocoa with the 2 cups flour. For the filling, substitute ¼ cup miniature chocolate chips for the nuts and use brown sugar.

CINNAMON ROLLS
Prepare as directed—except omit caramel topping and pecan halves. Grease bottom and sides of 13x9-inch pan with shortening or cooking spray. Place dough slices in pan. Let rise and bake as directed in steps 6 and 7—except do not turn pan upside down. Remove rolls from pan to cooling rack. Cool 10 minutes. Drizzle rolls with Vanilla Glaze: In medium saucepan, melt ½ cup butter over low heat. Stir in 2 cups powdered sugar and 1½ teaspoons vanilla. Stir in hot water, 1 tablespoon at a time, until glaze has the consistency of thick syrup.

MAPLE-PECAN ROLLS
Prepare Cinnamon Rolls (just above) as directed—except leave pecan pieces in the filling. For the Vanilla Glaze, substitute hot real maple syrup for the hot water.

ORANGE-PECAN STICKY ROLLS
Prepare as directed—except for the topping: Increase brown sugar to ¾ cup, decrease corn syrup to 2 tablespoons and add ⅓ cup orange marmalade. In small bowl, mix topping ingredients (do not heat), pour into pan and sprinkle with pecan halves. Omit filling. Spread ⅔ cup orange marmalade over the dough before rolling and cutting in step 5. Continue as directed.

STREUSEL-TOPPED CINNAMON ROLLS
Prepare Cinnamon Rolls (above) as directed—except in medium bowl, mix 1 cup all-purpose flour, ½ cup packed brown sugar, ¼ cup finely chopped cold butter and ¾ cup chopped nuts until crumbly. Sprinkle streusel evenly over rolls before baking.

Baking Powder
BISCUITS

12 BISCUITS   PREP TIME: **10 MINUTES**   START TO FINISH: **25 MINUTES**

2 cups all-purpose or whole wheat flour

1 tablespoon sugar

1 tablespoon baking powder

1 teaspoon salt

½ cup shortening or cold butter, cut into 8 pieces

¾ cup milk

1. Heat oven to 450°F. In medium bowl, mix flour, sugar, baking powder and salt. Cut in shortening, using pastry blender or fork, until mixture looks like fine crumbs. Stir in milk until dough leaves side of bowl.

2. Place dough on lightly floured surface. Knead lightly 10 times. Roll or pat dough until ½ inch thick. Cut with floured 2- to 2¼-inch biscuit cutter. On ungreased cookie sheet, place biscuits about 1 inch apart for crusty sides, or touching for soft sides.

3. Bake 10 to 12 minutes or until golden brown. Immediately remove from cookie sheet to cooling rack. Serve warm.

1 BISCUIT: CALORIES 160; TOTAL FAT 9G (SATURATED FAT 2.5G, TRANS FAT 1.5G); CHOLESTEROL 0MG; SODIUM 330MG; TOTAL CARBOHYDRATE 18G (DIETARY FIBER 0G); PROTEIN 3G **EXCHANGES:** 1 STARCH, 2 FAT **CARBOHYDRATE CHOICES:** 1

Techniques

SECRETS TO LIGHT AND FLUFFY BISCUITS

See Using the Right Pan (page 181).

See Measuring Ingredients (page 195).

WORKING WITH BISCUIT DOUGH

- When mixed, biscuit dough will be soft and sticky. If making rolled biscuits, more flour will be added when kneading, making the dough easier to cut with a biscuit cutter.
- Biscuits can be rolled and cut with a 2- to 2¼-inch biscuit cutter (dipped in flour each time before cutting) or dropped onto a cookie sheet. (See Drop Biscuit variation, page 209.)
- Stir only until the dough leaves the side of the bowl. Overmixing can cause the biscuits to be low volume and tough.
- Placing the cut biscuits so they touch each other will create biscuits with soft sides. Placing biscuits about an inch apart will create crusty sides.
- Remove the biscuits from the cookie sheet to a cooling rack immediately after baking to avoid them sticking to the pan.

VARIATIONS ▶

BAKING POWDER BISCUITS (CONTINUED)

Variations

BACON-CHEDDAR BISCUITS
Prepare as directed—except stir ½ cup shredded Cheddar cheese and ⅓ cup crisply cooked and crumbled bacon into the flour mixture before adding the milk.

BREAKFAST BISCUIT SANDWICHES
Prepare as directed—except use 3-inch cutter (yield will be 6 biscuits). Split biscuits in half while still warm. Spread with mayonnaise and mustard if desired. On each biscuit bottom, place 1 large sausage patty or 2 links cooked breakfast sausage or 2 links, ½ cup scrambled eggs and 1 slice American cheese; cover with biscuit tops. Serve immediately.

BUTTERMILK BISCUITS
Prepare as directed—except decrease baking powder to 2 teaspoons and add ¼ teaspoon baking soda with the sugar. Substitute buttermilk for the milk.

DROP BISCUITS
Prepare as directed—except increase milk to 1 cup. Grease cookie sheet with shortening. Drop dough in 12 spoonfuls about 2 inches apart onto cookie sheet.

SPICY CORNMEAL BISCUITS
Prepare as directed—except decrease flour to 1½ cups and add ¾ cup cornmeal with the flour. Reduce salt to ¼ teaspoon. Mix 1 cup shredded Monterey Jack cheese with jalapeños in with the flour mixture before adding the milk. Increase milk to 1 cup.

CORNBREAD

16 SERVINGS   PREP TIME: **10 MINUTES**   START TO FINISH: **10 MINUTES**

1   cup milk

¼   cup butter, melted

1   egg

1¼   cups yellow, white or blue cornmeal

1   cup all-purpose flour

½   cup sugar

3   teaspoons baking powder

½   teaspoon salt

1. Heat oven to 400°F. Grease bottom and side(s) of 9-inch round or 8-inch square pan or 8-inch cast-iron skillet with shortening or cooking spray.

2. In large bowl, beat milk, butter and egg with whisk. Add remaining ingredients all at once and stir just until flour is moistened (batter will be lumpy). Pour into pan.

3. Bake 20 to 25 minutes or until golden brown and toothpick inserted in center comes out clean. Serve warm if desired.

1 SERVING: CALORIES 170; TOTAL FAT 5G (SATURATED FAT 2.5G, TRANS FAT 0G); CHOLESTEROL 30MG; SODIUM 260MG; TOTAL CARBOHYDRATE 29G (DIETARY FIBER 0G); PROTEIN 4G **EXCHANGES:** 1 STARCH, 1 OTHER CARBOHYDRATE, 1 FAT **CARBOHYDRATE CHOICES:** 2

Cornbread is a natural with chili. Try it as a side to any grilled meat. Use leftovers to make Cornbread-Sausage Stuffing (page 155).

MAKING GREAT CORNBREAD

- See Measuring Ingredients, page 195.
- Cornmeal comes in yellow, white or blue depending on the type of corn used. All colors of cornmeal taste about the same, but the color of the cornbread will be different based on the color used. Use whatever color you prefer or have on hand.
- Cornmeal can be purchased ground or coarsely ground. Either can be used; however, the coarse-ground cornmeal will give the cornbread a bumpier texture, adding a bit of grit when eaten. Use whatever type you prefer or have on hand.
- Mix the batter just until the flour is moistened. The batter will still be lumpy, but the baked cornbread won't have lumps.
- If the batter is stirred too much, the resulting cornbread will have an unattractive peak on the top.
- Several types of pans can be used to bake cornbread. Choose from a square pan, round pan or cast-iron skillet, or make the cornbread into muffins (see Corn Muffins variation, page 213).
- Cast-iron skillets are a great choice (if you have one) because they hold the heat like no other pan, creating a delicious, crunchy crust.
- Be sure to check if the cornbread is done both by color and by using a toothpick. Start with the minimum bake time. Test, then add additional time, if needed.

VARIATIONS ▶

Variations

BACON AND SWISS CORNBREAD
Prepare as directed—except add 1 cup shredded Swiss cheese, ½ cup finely chopped onion and 4 slices crisply cooked and crumbled bacon with the flour.

CHEESE AND CHILES CORNBREAD
Prepare as directed—except stir in 1 cup shredded Cheddar cheese and 1 can (4.5 ounces) undrained chopped green chiles with the flour.

CORN MUFFINS
Prepare as directed—except grease bottoms only of 12 regular-size muffin cups with shortening or cooking spray. Divide batter evenly among muffin cups. Bake as directed.

PESTO CORNBREAD
Prepare as directed—except substitute ⅓ cup prepared pesto for the melted butter.

MAPLE BUTTER SPREAD FOR CORNBREAD
In small bowl, mix ½ cup softened butter and 1 tablespoon real maple syrup. Serve with cornbread.

Classic
FRENCH BREAD

2 LOAVES (12 SLICES EACH)   PREP TIME: **15 MINUTES**
START TO FINISH: **3 HOURS 5 MINUTES**

3 to 3½ cups all-purpose or bread flour

1 tablespoon sugar

1½ teaspoons salt

1 package regular or fast-acting dry yeast
(2¼ teaspoons)

1 cup very warm water (120°F to 130°F)

2 tablespoons vegetable oil

Cornmeal

1 egg white

1 tablespoon cold water

1. In large bowl, mix 2 cups flour, the sugar, salt and yeast. Add warm water and oil. Beat with electric mixer on low speed 1 minute, scraping bowl frequently. Beat on medium speed 1 minute, scraping bowl frequently. Stir in enough of remaining flour, ½ cup at a time, to make dough easy to handle (dough will be soft).

2. On lightly floured surface, knead dough about 5 minutes or until smooth and elastic. Grease large bowl with shortening or spray with cooking spray. Place dough in bowl, turning dough to grease all sides. Cover bowl loosely with plastic wrap and let rise in warm place 1 hour 30 minutes to 2 hours or until dough has doubled in size. (Rising time is longer than for traditional breads, which gives the typical French bread texture.) Dough is ready if indentation remains when dough is touched.

3. Grease large cookie sheet with shortening or spray with cooking spray; sprinkle with cornmeal. Turn dough out onto lightly floured surface; divide in half. Roll each half into 15x8-inch rectangle. Roll dough up tightly, beginning at 15-inch side, to form a loaf. Pinch edge of dough into roll to seal. Pinch ends under to seal, then shape ends to taper. Place both loaves seam side down on cookie sheet. With sharp or serrated knife, cut ¼-inch-deep slashes across tops of loaves at 2-inch intervals. Spray plastic wrap with cooking spray; cover loaves loosely.

4. Let rise in warm place about 1 hour or until dough has doubled in size. Place 8- or 9-inch square pan on bottom oven rack; add hot water to pan to about ½ inch from top. Heat oven to 375°F.

5. In small bowl, mix egg white and 1 tablespoon cold water; brush over loaves. Bake 18 to 20 minutes or until loaves are golden brown and sound hollow when tapped. Remove from cookie sheet to cooling rack; cool.

1 SLICE: CALORIES 70; TOTAL FAT 1.5G (SATURATED FAT 0G, TRANS FAT 0G); CHOLESTEROL 0MG; SODIUM 150MG; TOTAL CARBOHYDRATE 13G (DIETARY FIBER 0G); PROTEIN 2G **EXCHANGES:** 1 STARCH **CARBOHYDRATE CHOICES:** 1

Techniques

MAKING BAKERY-WORTHY FRENCH BREAD
See Measuring Ingredients (page 195).
See Working with Yeast (page 199).
See Kneading Yeast Dough (page 203).

CORNMEAL ON THE COOKIE SHEET?
A small amount of cornmeal on the cookie sheet when baking yeast dough lifts the dough slightly off the pan so that air can get underneath and bake the bread with a golden-brown crisp bottom crust.

TAPERING THE LOAF
Tapering the ends of the loaf means to shape them into a gradual narrowing. Tucking the ends under and tapering them gives the loaf the classic French bread shape.

SLASHING THE TOP
Making slashes helps control the shape of the loaf by giving it a place to expand while rising and baking.

A PAN OF HOT WATER
Placing a pan of hot water in your oven will create a great crust on the bread and imitate what commercial bread ovens can do when baking French bread.

VARIATIONS ▶

Variations

BREAD MACHINE FRENCH BREAD

Place 3½ cups all-purpose or bread flour, the sugar, salt, yeast, water and oil in bread machine pan in the order recommended by the manufacturer. Select Dough/Manual cycle. Do not use delay cycle. Remove dough from pan using lightly floured hands. Cover and let rest 10 minutes on lightly floured surface. Continue as directed in step 3.

OLIVE-WALNUT FRENCH BREAD

Prepare as directed—except decrease salt to 1 teaspoon. Before stirring in additional flour in step 1, add ⅔ cup chopped drained pimento-stuffed olives and ⅔ cup chopped walnuts.

PESTO-PARMESAN FRENCH BREAD

Prepare as directed—except add ¼ cup prepared pesto with the water. After dough is beaten, stir in ¼ cup grated Parmesan cheese and enough of remaining flour to make dough easy to handle. Continue as directed.

SEEDED FRENCH BREAD

Prepare as directed—except sprinkle loaves with desired amounts of poppy seed and/or sesame seed after brushing with egg white and water.

WHOLE WHEAT FRENCH BREAD

Prepare as directed—except use 1½ cups whole wheat flour and 1½ cups all-purpose flour. Substitute maple syrup for the sugar.

CRUSTY HARD ROLLS

Prepare as directed—except grease large cookie sheet with shortening or spray with cooking spray; sprinkle with cornmeal. After deflating dough, divide into 12 equal parts. Shape each part into a ball; place on cookie sheet 2 inches apart. Brush rolls with cold water. Let rise uncovered about 1 hour or until dough has doubled in size. Heat oven to 425°F. In small bowl, mix egg white and 1 tablespoon cold water; brush over rolls. Sprinkle with poppy seed or sesame seed. Bake 15 to 20 minutes or until brown.

Chewy
SOURDOUGH BREAD

1 LOAF (12 SLICES)   PREP TIME: **15 MINUTES**   START TO FINISH: **3 HOURS 20 MINUTES**

SOURDOUGH STARTER

1½	teaspoons regular or fast-acting active dry yeast
4	cups warm water (110°F to 115°F)
3	cups all-purpose flour
4	teaspoons sugar

BREAD

½	cup warm water (110°F to 115°F)
1	tablespoon sugar
½	teaspoons salt
1	teaspoon regular active or fast-acting dry yeast
2 to 3¼	cups all-purpose flour
1	teaspoon cornmeal

1. Make sourdough starter at least 1 week before making bread. In large glass bowl, dissolve 1½ teaspoons yeast in warm water. Stir in 3 cups flour and 4 teaspoons sugar. Beat with electric mixer on medium speed about 1 minute or until smooth. Cover loosely with towel or cheesecloth; let stand at room temperature about 1 week or until mixture is bubbly and has a sour aroma. Transfer to 2-quart or larger nonmetal bowl. Cover tightly; refrigerate until ready to use.

2. Use and replenish sourdough starter once a week, or stir in 1 teaspoon sugar. After using starter, replenish it by stirring in ¾ cup all-purpose flour, ¾ cup warm water and 1 teaspoon sugar until smooth. Cover loosely; let stand in warm place at least 1 day or until bubbly. Cover tightly; refrigerate until ready to use. To use, stir cold starter; measure cold starter and let stand until room temperature (starter will expand as it warms up).

3. In large bowl, mix 1 cup sourdough starter, ½ cup warm water, 1 tablespoon sugar, the salt, 1 teaspoon yeast and enough flour until dough is soft and leaves side of bowl. Place dough on lightly floured surface; knead 5 to 10 minutes or until dough is smooth and springy. Grease large bowl with oil. Place dough in bowl, turning dough to grease all sides. Cover bowl loosely with plastic wrap; let rise in warm place about 1 hour or until doubled in size. Dough is ready if indentation remains when dough is touched.

4. Line cookie sheet with cooking parchment paper and sprinkle center with cornmeal. Gently push fist into dough to deflate. Shape dough into ball by tightly pulling edges under to form smooth top. Place on cookie sheet and press dough to flatten slightly. Cover with plastic wrap that has been sprayed with cooking spray and let rise in warm place 45 minutes or until doubled in size.

5. Heat oven to 400°F. Using small strainer, sprinkle 1 teaspoon flour over top of dough. Using sharp serrated knife, cut 2 (¼-inch-deep) slashes on top of loaf, then make 2 crosswise cuts to create crisscross pattern.

6. Bake 25 to 30 minutes or until golden brown and loaf sounds hollow when tapped. Cool completely on cooling rack, about 1 hour.

1 SLICE: CALORIES 150; TOTAL FAT 0G (SATURATED FAT 0G, TRANS FAT 0G); CHOLESTEROL 0MG; SODIUM 300MG; TOTAL CARBOHYDRATE 32G (DIETARY FIBER 1G); PROTEIN 4G **EXCHANGES:** 1½ STARCH, ½ OTHER CARBOHYDRATE **CARBOHYDRATE CHOICES:** 2

Techniques

WHAT IS A SOURDOUGH STARTER?
A sourdough starter is a mixture of flour, water, yeast and sugar that is allowed to ferment at room temperature. It helps bread dough rise and contributes to a chewy, dense bread texture and the rich, complex, tangy taste of sourdough bread, which tastes amazing!

HOW TO MAKE A SOURDOUGH STARTER
Think of it as a kitchen pet. Treat your sourdough starter well, and it will provide you with great-tasting bread!
• Sourdough starters can be acidic, so store the starter in a glass bowl to avoid damaging metal bowls.
• You can use the starter as soon as it becomes bubbly (in about 1 week); however, we liked the flavor and texture of the bread even more when we used 2-week-old starter.
• Be sure to use or feed the starter as directed, or it won't have enough food to keep growing and could break down.
• Use and replenish the starter once a week or feed it regularly by adding a small amount of sugar. Or give some away to friends so that they can make their own sourdough bread. (Be sure to include the bread recipe here for them to use.)

VARIATIONS ▶

CHEWY SOURDOUGH BREAD (CONTINUED)

Variations

CHEESE FONDUE WITH SOURDOUGH
Prepare as directed. Cut cooled loaf into bite-size cubes to dip into your favorite cheese fondue as an appetizer or main dish.

GRILLED DILL-HAVARTI SOURDOUGH CROSTINI
Prepare as directed. Cut 8 slices of bread from loaf, ½ inch thick; cut slices crosswise in half. Brush one side of each slice lightly with olive oil; turn slices over. Sprinkle non-oiled sides of bread lightly with garlic powder (about 1 teaspoon for all slices) and 2 cups shredded Havarti cheese. Grill slices, oil side down, over medium heat 3 to 5 minutes or until bread is crisp and cheese is melted.

HERBED SOURDOUGH BREAD
Prepare as directed—except add 1 tablespoon each chopped fresh basil and oregano leaves and 2 teaspoons chopped fresh sage leaves with the sourdough starter in step 3.

WHOLE WHEAT SOURDOUGH BREAD
Prepare as directed—except substitute ¾ to 1¼ cups whole wheat flour for the all-purpose flour in step 3.

SOURDOUGH BOWL FOR DIPS
Use the sourdough loaf as an edible serving dish for dips. Cut a 1- to 2-inch slice from top of cooled loaf of bread. Hollow out loaf by cutting along edge with serrated knife, leaving about a 1-inch shell, and pulling out large chunks of bread. Cut or tear top slice and pulled-out bread into bite-size pieces. Place bread loaf on serving plate; fill with spinach, artichoke or other favorite dip. Arrange the bite-size bread pieces around loaf to use for dipping.

IMPRESSIVE

Desserts

49

Extraordinary CHOCOLATE CHIP COOKIES

6 DOZEN COOKIES   PREP TIME: **1 HOUR 25 MINUTES**   START TO FINISH: **1 HOUR 40 MINUTES**

1½	**cups butter, softened**
1¼	**cups granulated sugar**
1¼	**cups packed brown sugar**
1	**tablespoon vanilla**
2	**eggs**
4	**cups all-purpose flour**
2	**teaspoons baking soda**
½	**teaspoon salt**
1	**bag (24 oz) semisweet chocolate chips (4 cups)**

1. Heat oven to 350°F. In large bowl, beat butter, sugars, vanilla and eggs with electric mixer on medium speed or with spoon until light and fluffy. Stir in flour, baking soda and salt (dough will be stiff). Stir in chocolate chips.

2. Onto ungreased cookie sheet, drop dough by tablespoonfuls or #40 cookie/ice-cream scoop 2 inches apart. Flatten slightly.

3. Bake 11 to 13 minutes or until light brown (centers will be soft). Cool 1 to 2 minutes; remove from cookie sheet to cooling rack.

1 COOKIE: CALORIES 140; TOTAL FAT 7G (SATURATED FAT 4G, TRANS FAT 0G); CHOLESTEROL 15MG; SODIUM 85MG; TOTAL CARBOHYDRATE 18G (DIETARY FIBER 0G); PROTEIN 1G **EXCHANGES:** ½ STARCH, ½ OTHER CARBOHYDRATE, 1½ FAT **CARBOHYDRATE CHOICES:** 1

Techniques

MAKING AMAZING COOKIES
See Measuring Ingredients (page 195).

BUTTER KNOW-HOW
- Use real butter for best results and flavor when baking. If you substitute margarine, use those with at least 65 percent fat. Do not use reduced-fat butter or whipped products.
- Many recipes call for softened butter. The butter shouldn't be softened so much that it has melted spots. It will make the cookies spread too much and can negatively affect their texture.

SOFTENING BUTTER
For the most even results, soften butter at room temperature for 30 to 40 minutes. Or microwave the butter: Place unwrapped butter in microwavable glass bowl. Microwave uncovered on Low (30%): ½ to 1 cup butter will take 30 seconds to 1 minute.

COOKIE SHEETS

- Choose cookie sheets that are at least 2 inches smaller than the inside of your oven to allow the heat to circulate.
- Cookie sheets may be open on one to three sides. Jelly roll pans (15x10x1 inch) have four sides. They can also be used for cookies; however, it's harder to get the cookies off these pans without changing the shape of the cookies because of the sides.
- Owning at least 2 cookie sheets is helpful. While one batch is baking, prep the second batch.
- Use completely cooled cookie sheets to prevent cookies from spreading too much.

SUCCESSFUL BAKING

- Our pan choice for the nicest-looking cookies is shiny aluminum with a smooth surface. These pans reflect heat, allowing the cookies to bake evenly and brown properly.
- Insulated cookie sheets are intended to prevent cookies from browning too quickly, so cookies baked on these sheets may take longer to bake and may need to cool on the sheet a minute or two longer so that they can be removed without being damaged.
- Nonstick and dark-surface cookie sheets may cause cookies to be smaller in diameter and more rounded than if baked on shiny aluminum pans. The tops and especially the bottoms will be more browned and hard. To avoid over-browning and burning, check the manufacturer's instructions; some recommend reducing the oven temperature by 25°F. Also be sure to check cookies at the minimum bake time, then add more time if necessary.
- Bake the cookies in the middle of the oven. For even baking, make all the cookies the same size (see Cookie Scoops, page 227), and bake one sheet of cookies at a time. If you bake two sheets at once, position the racks as close to the center of the oven as possible, and rotate the position of the sheets halfway through baking.

GREASING PANS

- Grease pans as directed in recipe. High-fat cookies don't need the additional grease on the cookie sheets.
- Use only shortening or cooking spray for greasing as butter or butter substitutes can burn in the spaces between the cookies.

(continued on page 227)

TECHNIQUES AND VARIATIONS ▶

EXTRAORDINARY CHOCOLATE CHIP COOKIES (CONTINUED)

COOKIE SCOOPS

- The easiest and quickest way to ensure cookies are the same size and are perfectly shaped is to use a spring-handled scoop for placing the dough on the cookie sheet.
- To use the right size scoop, check the amount of dough each cookie is supposed to be in the recipe. Measure that much water into a scoop—if it fills it to the brim, it's the correct size scoop for the recipe.

BAKE A TEST COOKIE

- Bake one cookie before committing to baking the entire batch. You can adjust the dough if needed before baking the rest of it.
- If your cookie spreads too much, add 1 to 2 tablespoons additional flour to the dough, or refrigerate the dough 1 to 2 hours before baking.
- If the cookie is too round or hard, add 1 to 2 tablespoons milk to the dough.

Variations

CANDY COOKIES: Prepare as directed—except substitute 4 cups candy-coated chocolate candies for the chocolate chips.

CHOCOLATE CHIP COOKIE 'WICHES: Prepare as directed. Sandwich the flat sides of two baked cookies with ice cream (any flavor) in-between. Roll edge in sprinkles, if desired. Wrap in plastic wrap and freeze 1 to 2 hours or until firm.

MINT CHOCOLATE CHIP COOKIES: Prepare as directed—except add ½ to 1 teaspoon mint extract and 12 to 16 drops green food color with the eggs. Substitute 2 cups crème de menthe baking chips for 2 cups of the chocolate chips.

PEANUT BUTTER–CHOCOLATE CHIP COOKIES: Prepare as directed—except substitute 2 cups candy-coated peanut butter–milk chocolate chips or peanut butter baking chips for 2 cups of the chocolate chips.

WHOLE WHEAT CHOCOLATE CHIP COOKIES: Prepare as directed—except substitute 1½ cups whole wheat flour for 1½ cups of the all-purpose flour.

50

Classic SUGAR COOKIES

5 DOZEN (2-INCH) COOKIES   PREP TIME: **1 HOUR**   START TO FINISH: **3 HOURS 10 MINUTES**

COOKIES

1½	**cups powdered sugar**
1	**cup butter, softened**
1	**teaspoon vanilla**
½	**teaspoon almond extract**
1	**egg**
2½	**cups all-purpose flour**
1	**teaspoon baking soda**
1	**teaspoon cream of tartar**

DECORATOR'S GLAZE

2	**cups powdered sugar**
2	**tablespoons water**
2	**tablespoons light corn syrup**
½	**teaspoon almond extract**
	Food colors, if desired
	Colored sugar, if desired

1. In large bowl, mix powdered sugar, butter, vanilla, almond extract and egg. Stir in remaining ingredients for cookies. Cover and refrigerate at least 2 hours.

2. Heat oven to 375°F. Lightly grease cookie sheet with shortening or cooking spray.

3. Divide dough in half. Roll each half until ¼ inch thick on lightly floured surface. Cut into desired shapes with 2- to 2½-inch cookie cutters. Place on cookie sheet 2 inches apart.

4. Bake 7 to 8 minutes or until edges are light brown. Remove from cookie sheet to cooling rack.

5. In small bowl, beat all glaze ingredients except food colors and colored sugar with electric mixer on low speed until smooth. Divide evenly among several small bowls. Stir desired food color, one drop at a time, into each bowl until desired color. Decorate cookies with glaze and colored sugar.

1 COOKIE: CALORIES 80; TOTAL FAT 3G (SATURATED FAT 2G, TRANS FAT 0G); CHOLESTEROL 10MG; SODIUM 45MG; TOTAL CARBOHYDRATE 12G (DIETARY FIBER 0G); PROTEIN 0G **EXCHANGES:** ½ STARCH, ½ OTHER CARBOHYDRATE, ½ FAT **CARBOHYDRATE CHOICES:** 1

Techniques

See Measuring Ingredients (page 195).

SUCCESSFULLY ROLLING AND CUTTING COOKIES
- Refrigerate the cookie dough as directed in the recipe to make it not sticky when rolling.
- Working with half of the dough at a time keeps it from warming up and getting sticky.
- Flour the surface and rolling pin lightly to help prevent sticking.
- Find two sticks, clean rulers, etc., of the same thickness that the recipe directs the dough to be rolled to. Place one stick on each side of the dough just far enough apart that the edges of your rolling pin can still roll on top of them. Roll out the dough until it's as thick as the sticks (you won't be able to roll it any thinner while using the sticks).
- Dip cutters in flour and tap off excess if dough sticks to the cutters.

DECORATE-BEFORE-YOU-BAKE COOKIES
Prepare Classic Sugar Cookies as directed—except omit the Decorator's Glaze.
Decorate cookies before baking with any of these methods:
- Sprinkle with granulated or colored sugar.
- **Egg Yolk Paint**: In small bowl, mix 1 egg yolk and ¼ teaspoon water. Divide mixture among several custard cups. Tint each with a different food color. Brush onto unbaked cookies.
- **Baked-On Decorating Mixture**: In small bowl, mix ½ cup each softened butter and all-purpose flour and 1 tablespoon milk until well mixed. Divide mixture in half; tint each half with 4 drops food color. Place mixtures in decorating bags fitted with small writing tips. Pipe onto unbaked cookies.

VARIATIONS ▶

Variations

ALMOND SUGAR COOKIES

Prepare as directed—except subtitute almond extract for the vanilla.

CHOCOLATE-DIPPED SUGAR COOKIES

Prepare as directed—except omit Decorator's Glaze. In small microwavable bowl, microwave 1⅓ cups semisweet chocolate chips and 1 tablespoon shortening uncovered on High 1 to 1½ minutes or until mixture is melted and can be stirred until smooth. Dip half of each cookie into melted chocolate. Place on waxed paper; let stand until chocolate is set, about 30 minutes. Or, if stacking cookies for storage, let stand 1½ hours to set completely. Store in airtight container.

CONFETTI SUGAR COOKIES

Prepare as directed—except stir 2 tablespoons confetti sprinkles with the flour. Substitute additional confetti sprinkles for the colored sugar when glazing the cookies.

JAM-SANDWICH SUGAR COOKIES

Prepare as directed—except omit Decorator's Glaze. Spread about 2 teaspoons any flavor jam on the flat side of half of the baked and cooled sugar cookies. Top with remaining sugar cookies, flat side down.

SWIRLED SUGAR COOKIES

Prepare as directed—except omit Decorator's Glaze. Frost each cookie with decorator's icing from a tube. Pipe 4 or 5 small dots red, green or blue cookie icing or decorating gel onto top of each cookie, and immediately swirl color with toothpick to create marbled designs.

#51

Killer
CANDY BAR BROWNIES

24 BROWNIES   PREP TIME: **35 MINUTES**   START TO FINISH: **3 HOURS 15 MINUTES**

BROWNIES

- ²/₃ **cup butter**
- 5 **oz unsweetened baking chocolate, chopped (from two 4-oz boxes)**
- 1³/₄ **cups granulated sugar**
- 3 **eggs**
- 2 **teaspoons vanilla**
- 1 **cup all-purpose flour**
- ³/₄ **cup mini peanut butter cups (from 8-oz bag)**
- ½ **cup chocolate-covered caramels (from 12-oz bag), unwrapped**

PEANUT BUTTER FROSTING

- ½ **cup butter, softened**
- ½ **cup creamy peanut butter**
- 1 **teaspoon vanilla**
- 2½ **cups powdered sugar**
- 2 to 3 **tablespoons milk**
- ¼ **cup candy-coated chocolate candies (from 10.7-oz bag)**

1. Heat oven to 350°F. Spray 9-inch square pan with cooking spray.

2. In 1-quart saucepan, melt ²/₃ cup butter and the chocolate over low heat, stirring constantly, until melted. Remove from heat: cool 5 minutes.

3. Meanwhile, in medium bowl, beat granulated sugar, eggs and 2 teaspoons vanilla with electric mixer on high speed 5 minutes. Beat in chocolate mixture on low speed, scraping bowl occasionally. Beat in flour just until well blended, scraping bowl occasionally. Stir in peanut butter cups until well mixed; spread evenly in pan. Sprinkle with chocolate-covered caramels, slightly pressing into batter.

4. Bake 35 to 40 minutes or until toothpick inserted 1 inch from edge of pan comes out almost clean. Cool completely, about 2 hours.

5. In medium bowl, beat ½ cup butter, the peanut butter and 1 teaspoon vanilla with electric mixer on high speed 1 to 2 minutes or until creamy. Add powdered sugar, 1 cup at a time, until well blended. Beat in milk, 1 tablespoon at a time, until spreading consistency. Spread evenly over brownies. Sprinkle with candy-coated chocolate candies. Cut into 4 rows x 6 rows. Store covered in refrigerator.

1 BROWNIE: CALORIES 360; TOTAL FAT 19G (SATURATED FAT 10G, TRANS FAT 0G); CHOLESTEROL 50MG; SODIUM 130MG; TOTAL CARBOHYDRATE 42G (DIETARY FIBER 1G); PROTEIN 4G **EXCHANGES:** 1½ STARCH, 1½ OTHER CARBOHYDRATE, 3½ FAT **CARBOHYDRATE CHOICES:** 3

BROWNIE BAKING SECRETS

- See Measuring Ingredients (page 195).
- See Using the Right Pan (page 181).
- **Cool the chocolate mixture only 5 minutes,** or the mixture may not be warm enough to dissolve the sugar, producing grainy brownies when baked.
- **Use the exact size pan** called for when baking bars such as brownies. Bars made in pans that are too big become hard and overcooked, and those made in pans that are too small can be doughy and raw in the center and hard on the edges.
- Place pans in the middle of the oven to bake.
- **Check the bars at the minimum time,** using the doneness indicator indicated in the recipe (in this case, a toothpick inserted 1 inch from the edge of the pan). If the bars are not done, bake a few minutes longer or until they pass the doneness test.
- Cool the brownies in the pan on a cooling rack.
- Use a plastic knife to cut brownies for the nicest edges.

ADDING CANDY TO BROWNIES

We've added three types of chocolate candies to this recipe for an over-the-top decadent treat. You can experiment with other chocolate candies, keeping these guidelines in mind:

- Choose small candies or cut candies into small pieces before adding to the recipe.
- Some chewy candies become even chewier when baked. Choose chocolate or caramel-type candies that aren't very chewy right out of the bag.
- Heavier candies can sink to the bottom of the brownies if added to the batter. Placing them on top of the batter before baking allows them to sink into the brownies without sinking to the bottom of the pan.
- Another way to add candies to the brownies is to vary the candies that are added on top of the frosting. Try different varieties of chocolate or caramel-type candies, substituting ¼ cup small or cut-up candies for the candy-coated chocolate candies.

VARIATIONS ▶

KILLER CANDY BAR BROWNIES (CONTINUED)

Variations

BROWNIES FOR A CROWD
Prepare as directed—except spray 13x9-inch pan with cooking spray and double brownie ingredients. Bake 50 to 55 minutes. Cool and frost as directed, doubling frosting ingredients.

CANDY-BROWNIE ICE-CREAM SQUARES
Prepare as directed—except omit frosting. Spread cooled brownies with ½ gallon softened ice cream. Drizzle with chocolate or caramel topping. Sprinkle with desired candy. Cover and freeze 1 to 2 hours or until firm. Cut into squares.

COCONUT–PEANUT BUTTER CANDY BROWNIES
Prepare as directed—except decrease vanilla to 1½ teaspoons. Add ½ teaspoon coconut extract with the vanilla. Omit candy-coated chocolate candies. Immediately after frosting brownies, sprinkle with ½ cup coconut.

PEANUT BUTTER OVERLOAD BROWNIES
Prepare as directed—except substitute ⅓ cup crunchy peanut butter for ⅓ cup of the butter.

WHITE CHOCOLATE–ALMOND BROWNIES
Prepare as directed—except decrease vanilla to 1 teaspoon and add ½ teaspoon almond extract. Substitute white chocolate chips for the peanut butter cups and chopped almonds for the chocolate-covered caramels; stir into batter before spreading in pan. Omit frosting. Dust cooled brownies with powdered sugar.

Party-Ready
IN 30 MINUTES

Pull off a party from your pantry in about 30 minutes. Simply run through this simple checklist and start the fun!

☐ Heat the oven for frozen appetizers you keep on hand for impromptu entertaining. Many grocery stores and big-box stores have a good variety of high-quality options.

☐ Quickly dust and vacuum the party areas if necessary. Lower the lights if there's no time for cleaning.

☐ Check the bathroom for cleanliness; change the hand towel.

☐ Stash clutter.

☐ Put beverages on ice.

☐ Pull out snacks you have on hand: chips, popcorn, nuts, pickles, etc. Place in serving containers on the serving counter or table.

☐ Arrange plates, napkins, utensils and glasses on the serving area.

☐ Bake frozen appetizers.

☐ Select music from a free online channel or your music device.

☐ Light candles.

☐ Welcome guests and let the fun begin!

52

CHOCOLATE FUDGE

64 CANDIES   PREP TIME: **35 MINUTES**   START TO FINISH: **2 HOURS 35 MINUTES**

4   **cups sugar**

1⅓   **cups milk or half-and-half**

¼   **cup light corn syrup**

¼   **teaspoon salt**

4   **oz unsweetened baking chocolate, chopped**

¼   **cup butter, cut into pieces**

2   **teaspoons vanilla**

1   **cup chopped nuts, if desired**

1. Grease bottom and sides of 8-inch square pan with butter.

2. In heavy 3-quart saucepan, cook sugar, milk, corn syrup, salt and chocolate over medium heat, stirring constantly, until chocolate is melted and sugar is dissolved. Cook, stirring occasionally, to 234°F on candy thermometer or until small amount of mixture dropped into cup of very cold water forms a soft ball that flattens when removed from water; remove from heat. Stir in butter.

3. Cool mixture to 120°F without stirring, about 1 hour. (Bottom of saucepan will be lukewarm.) Add vanilla. Beat vigorously and continuously with wooden spoon 5 to 10 minutes or until mixture is thick and no longer glossy. (Mixture will hold its shape when dropped from a spoon.)

4. Quickly stir in nuts. Spread in pan. Let stand about 1 hour or until firm. Cut into 1-inch squares. Store in airtight container.

1 CANDY: CALORIES 70; TOTAL FAT 1.5G (SATURATED FAT 1G, TRANS FAT 0G); CHOLESTEROL 0MG; SODIUM 20MG; TOTAL CARBOHYDRATE 14G (DIETARY FIBER 0G); PROTEIN 0G **EXCHANGES:** 1 OTHER CARBOHYDRATE, ½ FAT **CARBOHYDRATE CHOICES:** 1

Techniques

CHOOSING THE RIGHT PAN

- Use the exact size saucepan called for in the recipe or the cooking time will be affected.
- Use the size and material of pan called for in the recipe so the candy will have the right thickness and texture and will set up properly.

MIXING, COOKING AND COOLING CANDY

- For best results, use butter. If you use margarine, it needs to be at least 65 percent fat. Do not use vegetable oil spreads or reduced-fat or tub products.
- Don't double a candy recipe. Increasing the amount of ingredients can change the cooking time, so the candy may not set up properly. Make two batches instead.

- A cool, dry day is best for making candy as the candy may struggle to set up properly on a humid day.
- Unless otherwise directed, don't stir the candy mixture while it is cooling. Stirring while cooling can cause the mixture to crystallize, resulting in a grainy candy. Follow the recipe exactly, stirring only when indicated.

USING A CANDY THERMOMETER

Check the accuracy of your candy thermometer before starting the recipe.

1. Put the thermometer into a pan of water and bring the water to a boil. The thermometer should read 212°F (unless you live in a high-altitude area).
2. If it doesn't, note how much higher or lower the temperature reads than 212°F, then make the adjustment to the temperature needed in the recipe you are making.

- If you live in a high-altitude area (above 3,500 feet), refer to an altitude table to find out the boiling point, and adjust the temperature needed in the recipe you are making.
- To get an accurate reading, the thermometer should stand upright in the candy mixture, with the bulb or tip submerged in the candy mixture but not resting on the bottom of the pan.
- Read the thermometer at eye level.
- Watch the temperature closely—after 200°F, it goes up very quickly.
- If you don't have a candy thermometer, use the cold-water test, in which a small amount of the candy mixture is dropped into a cupful of very cold water (see Testing Candy Temperatures below).

TESTING CANDY TEMPERATURES

Soft-ball stage (234°F to 240°F): When dropped into very cold water, forms a soft ball that flattens between fingers.

VARIATIONS ▶

Variations

CHERRY-CHOCOLATE FUDGE
Prepare as directed—except stir in ½ cup dried cherries with the nuts.

MOCHA-NUT FUDGE
Prepare as directed—except add 4 teaspoons instant coffee powder with the chocolate.

PENUCHE
Prepare as directed—except substitute 2 cups packed brown sugar for 2 cups of the granulated sugar, and omit baking chocolate.

PEPPERMINT-TOPPED FUDGE
Prepare as directed—except after spreading fudge mixture in pan, immediately sprinkle with ¼ cup crushed peppermint candies; press lightly.

TOFFEE-CHOCOLATE FUDGE
Prepare as directed—except substitute 1 cup toffee bits for the nuts.

#53

Peaches and Cream
SHORTCAKES

8 SERVINGS   PREP TIME: **40 MINUTES**   START TO FINISH: **1 HOUR 20 MINUTES**

SHORTCAKES

2	cups all-purpose flour
¼	cup plus 1 tablespoon granulated sugar
2	teaspoons baking powder
½	teaspoon salt
¼	teaspoon baking soda
½	cup cold butter, cut into pieces
¾	cup cold buttermilk
1	egg, slightly beaten

FILLING

4	cups peeled sliced fresh peaches (4 to 5 medium)
¼	cup granulated sugar
1	teaspoon ground cinnamon

SWEETENED WHIPPED CREAM

1	cup heavy whipping cream
3	tablespoons powdered sugar
½	teaspoon vanilla

1. Heat oven to 375°F. Line large cookie sheet with cooking parchment paper.

2. In large bowl, mix flour, ¼ cup granulated sugar, the baking powder, salt and baking soda. Cut in butter, using pastry blender or fork, until mixture looks like coarse crumbs. Stir in buttermilk and egg just until blended. (Do not overmix.)

3. Using ⅓-cup measuring cup, drop dough to form 8 shortcakes about 2 inches apart onto cookie sheet. Sprinkle tops of shortcakes with remaining 1 tablespoon granulated sugar. Bake 14 to 18 minutes or until golden brown. Remove from cookie sheet to cooling rack; cool completely, about 20 minutes.

4. In large bowl, mix peaches, ¼ cup granulated sugar and the cinnamon until well coated. In chilled medium bowl, beat whipping cream with electric mixer on medium-high speed until slightly thickened. Reduce speed to low; beat in powdered sugar and vanilla. Increase speed; beat mixture until stiff peaks form.

5. Split shortcakes in half horizontally. Spoon filling and whipped cream between halves; replace tops. Top with additional filling and whipped cream.

1 SERVING: CALORIES 450; TOTAL FAT 24G (SATURATED FAT 15G, TRANS FAT 1G); CHOLESTEROL 90MG; SODIUM 440MG; TOTAL CARBOHYDRATE 51G (DIETARY FIBER 2G); PROTEIN 6G **EXCHANGES:** 2 STARCH, 1½ OTHER CARBOHYDRATE, 4 ½ FAT **CARBOHYDRATE CHOICES:** 3½

Techniques

- See Baking Powder Biscuit Techniques (page 207).
- Spray the measuring cup with cooking spray to prevent the dough from sticking when you're dropping it onto cookie sheet.

LEARN TO BLANCH

Blanching is quick way to peel the peaches. Use this method and it will be super-easy to remove the peel with a paring knife or your fingers:

- Fill a large pot with water and bring to a boil.
- Immerse peaches in boiling water about 15 seconds.
- Remove from water with a slotted spoon or small strainer, and immediately plunge them into a bowl of ice water to stop the cooking process.
- Drain well. When cooled, use a paring knife or your fingers to remove skin. (If the skins aren't coming off easily, repeat the process, plunging peaches back into boiling water for another 5 to 10 seconds.)
- Slice peaches and remove pits.

VARIATIONS ▶

Variations

BLUEBERRY-ORANGE SHORTCAKES
Prepare as directed—except add 2 teaspoons grated orange zest with the sugar in the shortcakes. Before baking, mix 1 tablespoon sugar and 1 tablespoon grated orange zest; sprinkle over shortcakes. Substitute 4 cups blueberries for the peaches.

CHOCOLATE CHIP–STRAWBERRY SHORTCAKES
Prepare as directed—except stir in ½ cup miniature chocolate chips before stirring in buttermilk and egg. Substitute 4 cups sliced fresh strawberries for the peaches. Omit cinnamon.

COCONUT-MANGO SHORTCAKES
Prepare as directed—except add ⅔ cup toasted flake coconut before stirring in buttermilk and egg. Substitute 4 cups cubed fresh mango for the peaches.

PEACH AND MAPLE-CREAM SHORTCAKES
Prepare as directed—except substitute Maple Cream for the Sweetened Whipped Cream: In small bowl, beat ⅓ cup heavy whipping cream and 2 tablespoons powdered sugar with electric mixer on high speed until soft peaks form. Gently fold in 1 container (6 ounces) vanilla yogurt and ¾ teaspoon maple flavor. Refrigerate until serving time.

RASPBERRY-PEACH SHORTCAKES
Prepare as directed—except substitute 2 cups fresh raspberries for 2 cups of the peaches.

CHOCOLATE LAYER CAKE

12 SERVINGS   PREP TIME: **20 MINUTES**   START TO FINISH: **2 HOURS 5 MINUTES**

2¼	cups all-purpose flour
1⅔	cups sugar
1¼	cups water
¾	cup butter, softened
⅔	cup unsweetened baking cocoa
1¼	teaspoons baking soda
1	teaspoon salt
¼	teaspoon baking powder
2	eggs
1	teaspoon vanilla
	Fudge Frosting (page 250), if desired

1. Heat oven to 350°F. Grease bottoms and sides of 2 (9-inch) or 3 (8-inch) round cake pans with shortening; lightly flour.

2. In large bowl, beat all ingredients except frosting with electric mixer on low speed 30 seconds, scraping bowl constantly. Beat on high speed 3 minutes, scraping bowl occasionally. Divide batter evenly between pans.

3. Bake 30 to 35 minutes or until toothpick inserted in center comes out clean. Cool 10 minutes; remove from pans to cooling racks. Cool completely, about 1 hour.

4. Fill and frost layers with frosting.

1 SERVING: CALORIES 330; TOTAL FAT 13G (SATURATED FAT 6G, TRANS FAT 0.5G); CHOLESTEROL 65MG; SODIUM 430MG; TOTAL CARBOHYDRATE 48G (DIETARY FIBER 2G); PROTEIN 5G **EXCHANGES:** 2 STARCH, 1 OTHER CARBOHYDRATE, 2½ FAT **CARBOHYDRATE CHOICES:** 3

Techniques

PREPPING FOR GREAT CAKES
See Measuring Ingredients (page 195).
See Butter Know-How (page 224).
See Using the Right Pan (page 181).

MEASURING PANS
If your pans aren't marked with their size on the bottom, be sure your pan is the right size by measuring it from inside edge to inside edge. Using the wrong size pan will affect the bake time and could affect the texture and height of the cake.

GREASING CAKE PANS
Grease pans with solid shortening, not butter or margarine, because those can burn. Use cooking spray if the recipe calls for it.

TIPS FOR CAKES WITH GREAT SHAPE AND STRUCTURE

- Be sure the oven is heated to the correct temperature before baking.
- Invest in an oven thermometer, and place it in the center of the oven to be sure your oven is calibrated correctly. Adjust the oven temperature until the thermometer reads what the recipe calls for.
- Avoid overmixing the batter, which can cause tunnels or a sunken center.

BAKING CAKES

- Bake cakes on the center rack with at least 1 inch of space between the pans and the sides of the oven.
- If not all the pans will fit on one rack, refrigerate those that don't fit until the others are baked, and then bake the remaining pans.
- For perfectly baked cakes, set the timer for the minimum time given in the recipe. Check for the doneness indicator called for in the recipe (usually either the toothpick test or touching the cake lightly with a finger to see if it springs back). If the cake isn't done, bake a little longer until the doneness indicator works.

COOLING AND PAN REMOVAL

Follow the directions in the recipe you are using for cake cooling and pan removal.

- To remove a cake from a pan, insert a knife between the cake and the pan, then slide the knife around edge to loosen the cake.

Place cooling rack upside down over cake. Carefully invert pan and cooling rack; remove pan.

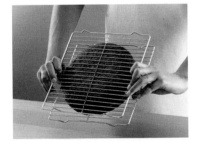

Place another cooling rack on top of cake. Invert cooling rack and cake again so that the cake is on second rack, right side up. Remove top cooling rack.

- If the cake wants to stick to the pan when you're trying to remove it, try reheating it in the oven for 1 minute and then remove the cake from the pan.
- Cool cakes on cooling racks to allow air circulation.

CUTTING CAKES

Use a thin, sharp knife with a gentle sawing motion to cut cakes without tearing or squishing.

VARIATIONS ▶

Variations

CHOCOLATE CAKE WITH STRAWBERRIES
Prepare as directed—except when frosting between the cake layers, top with sliced strawberries. Arrange whole strawberries on top of frosted cake.

CHOCOLATE SHEET CAKE
Grease bottom and sides of 13x9-inch pan with shortening; lightly flour. Prepare batter as directed; pour into pan. Bake 40 to 45 minutes or until toothpick inserted in center comes out clean. Cool completely in pan on cooling rack. Frost top of cake with frosting.

CHOCOLATE-CAPPUCCINO CAKE
Prepare as directed—except add 1 tablespoon instant espresso coffee powder, coffee granules or crystals and ½ teaspoon ground cinnamon with the cocoa. When making the Fudge Frosting, add an additional 2 teaspoons instant espresso coffee powder with the cocoa.

CHOCOLATE-CARAMEL CAKE
Prepare as directed—except substitute Caramel Frosting for the Fudge Frosting: In 2-quart saucepan, melt ½ cup butter over medium heat. Stir in 1 cup packed brown sugar. Heat to boiling, stirring constantly; reduce heat. Simmer and stir 2 minutes. Stir in ¼ cup milk. Heat to boiling; remove from heat. Cool to lukewarm, about 30 minutes. Gradually stir in 2 cups powdered sugar. Place saucepan of frosting in bowl of cold water. Beat with spoon until frosting is smooth and spreadable. Immediately fill and frost cake. Decorate top of cake with chewy caramels or chocolate-covered caramel candies, if desired.

TURTLE LAYER CAKE
Prepare as directed—except substitute Caramel Frosting (above) for the Fudge Frosting. After frosting first layer, press ½ cup coarsely chopped pecans gently into frosting on top of cake before topping with second layer. Sprinkle top of frosted cake with an additional ½ cup coarsely chopped pecans; press lightly into frosting.

#55

Fudge FROSTING

3½ CUPS FROSTING   PREP TIME: **10 MINUTES**   START TO FINISH: **55 MINUTES**

2 **cups granulated sugar**

1 **cup unsweetened baking cocoa**

1 **cup milk**

½ **cup butter, cut into pieces**

¼ **cup light corn syrup**

¼ **teaspoon salt**

2 **teaspoons vanilla**

2½ to 3 **cups powdered sugar**

1. In 3-quart saucepan, mix granulated sugar and cocoa. Stir in milk, butter, corn syrup and salt. Heat to boiling, stirring frequently. Boil 3 minutes, stirring occasionally. Remove from heat; cool 45 minutes.

2. Beat in vanilla and enough powdered sugar for spreading consistency.

3. Frost 13x9-inch cake, or fill and frost 8- or 9-inch two-layer cake. Leftover frosting can be tightly covered and refrigerated up to 5 days or frozen up to 1 month. Let stand 30 minutes at room temperature to soften; stir before using.

1 SERVING (ABOUT ¼ CUP): CALORIES 170; TOTAL FAT 4.5G (SATURATED FAT 3G, TRANS FAT 0G); CHOLESTEROL 10MG; SODIUM 35MG; TOTAL CARBOHYDRATE 32G (DIETARY FIBER 1G); PROTEIN 1G **EXCHANGES:** 2 OTHER CARBOHYDRATE, 1 FAT **CARBOHYDRATE CHOICES:** 2

Techniques

HOW TO FROST A LAYER CAKE

Place 4 strips of waxed paper around edge of plate. Brush away any loose crumbs from cooled cake layer; place rounded side down on plate.

Spread ¼ to ½ cup frosting over top of first layer to within ½ inch of edge. Place second cake layer (brushing away any loose crumbs as directed at left), rounded side up, on frosted first layer.

Coat side of cake with very thin layer of frosting to seal in crumbs. Frost side of cake in swirls, making a rim about ¼ inch high above top of cake.

Spread remaining frosting on top, just to the built-up rim. Carefully remove waxed paper strips.

Variations

FUDGE TOPPING: Prepare as directed. Place frosting in microwavable bowl. Microwave on High 10 to 15 seconds or until drizzling consistency. Immediately drizzle over angel food or pound cake, ice cream or fresh berries. (One cup frosting will be enough to top about 8 servings of dessert.)

MEXICAN FUDGE FROSTING: Prepare as directed—except add 1 tablespoon ground cinnamon and ¼ teaspoon ground red pepper (cayenne) with the granulated sugar.

MINT FUDGE FROSTING: Prepare as directed—except decrease vanilla to 1 teaspoon. Stir in ¼ to ½ teaspoon mint (not peppermint) extract with the vanilla. When cake is frosted, top cake with thin rectangular mint chocolate candies, either whole or coarsely chopped.

MOCHA FUDGE FROSTING: Prepare as directed—except add 1 tablespoon instant coffee granules or crystals with the granulated sugar.

FUDGE S'MORES: Prepare as directed. Spread frosting on one side of 2 graham cracker squares. Toast 1 or 2 marshmallows over a fire or hot grill; place between graham crackers, frosting side in.

#56

Classic
APPLE PIE

8 SERVINGS   PREP TIME: **30 MINUTES**   START TO FINISH: **3 HOURS 20 MINUTES**

Two-Crust Pastry (page 256)

½ cup plus 1 tablespoon sugar

¼ cup all-purpose flour

¾ teaspoon ground cinnamon

¼ teaspoon ground nutmeg

Dash salt

6 cups thinly sliced (⅛ inch thick) peeled tart apples (6 medium)

2 tablespoons cold butter, if desired

2 teaspoons water

1. Heat oven to 425°F. Place pastry in 9-inch glass pie plate.

2. In large bowl, mix ½ cup sugar, the flour, cinnamon, nutmeg and salt. Stir in apples. Spoon into pastry-lined pie plate. Cut butter into small pieces; sprinkle over apples. Cover with top pastry; cut slits in pastry. Seal and flute (see Pastry Edge Treatments, page 258).

3. Brush top crust with 2 teaspoons water; sprinkle with remaining 1 tablespoon sugar. Cover edge with pie crust shield ring or 2- to 3-inch strip of foil to prevent excessive browning; remove shield or foil during last 15 minutes of baking.

4. Bake 40 to 50 minutes or until crust is golden brown and juice begins to bubble through slits in crust. Cool on cooling rack at least 2 hours.

1 SERVING: CALORIES 420; TOTAL FAT 21G (SATURATED FAT 7G, TRANS FAT 2G); CHOLESTEROL 10MG; SODIUM 330MG; TOTAL CARBOHYDRATE 53G (DIETARY FIBER 3G); PROTEIN 4G **EXCHANGES:** 1½ STARCH, 2 FRUIT, 4 FAT **CARBOHYDRATE CHOICES:** 3½

CHOOSING THE BEST APPLES

- Choose local apples, if available. They will often be the freshest and juiciest.
- Not all apples are good apples for pie because of their sweetness and texture. Braeburn, Cortland, Granny Smith, Haralson and Jonathan are tart (perfect for apple pie) and bake up juicy but not mushy.
- Mix two or three varieties for best taste and texture.
- Cut apples thinly and evenly to ensure they cook all the way through.

PICKING PIE PANS

Choose heat-resistant glass pie plates for pies with the best texture and color.

FREEZING FILLED PIES

- Completely cool baked pies before freezing.
- Do not freeze cream, custard or meringue-topped pies. The filling and the meringue will break down and become watery.
- Freeze pies with space around them so that the pastry edge won't get broken or misshapen during freezing. Once they are frozen, other items can touch up against the pies.
- Fruit pies can be made ahead and frozen unbaked or baked. Pecan and pumpkin pies need to be baked before freezing.

THAWING FROZEN BAKED FRUIT AND PECAN PIES

- Thaw frozen baked fruit and pecan pies unwrapped at room temperature 1 hour before serving. Serve at room temperature or bake in 375°F oven 35 to 40 minutes or until warm.
- Thaw frozen baked pumpkin pies unwrapped 3 to 4 hours in refrigerator.

VARIATIONS ▶

CLASSIC APPLE PIE (CONTINUED)

Variations

BLUEBERRY PIE
Prepare as directed—except use 1¼ cups sugar and substitute ½ cup cornstarch for the flour. Decrease cinnamon to ½ teaspoon and omit nutmeg and salt. Substitute fresh blueberries for the sliced apples. Stir in 1 tablespoon fresh lemon juice with the blueberries. Decrease butter to 1 tablespoon. Bake pie 35 to 45 minutes or just until juices begin to bubble through crust.

CHERRY PIE
Prepare as directed—except use 1⅓ cups sugar and increase flour to ½ cup. Omit cinnamon, nutmeg and salt. Substitute 6 cups fresh pitted sour cherries for the apples. Bake pie 35 to 45 minutes or just until juices begin to bubble through crust.

CLASSIC PEACH PIE
Prepare as directed—except use ⅔ cup sugar and ⅓ cup flour. Decrease cinnamon to ¼ teaspoon and omit nutmeg. Substitute sliced peeled fresh peaches (6 to 8 medium) for the sliced apples. Stir in 1 teaspoon fresh lemon juice with the peaches. Decrease butter to 1 tablespoon. Bake pie 45 minutes or just until juices begin to bubble through crust.

FRENCH APPLE PIE
Prepare as directed—except heat oven to 400°F. Omit butter, 2 teaspoons water and 1 tablespoon sugar. In small bowl, mix 1 cup all-purpose flour and ½ cup packed brown sugar. Cut in ½ cup cold butter with fork until crumbly. Sprinkle over apple mixture. Bake 35 to 40 minutes or until golden brown.

STRAWBERRY-RHUBARB PIE
Prepare as directed—except use 2 cups sugar and increase flour to ½ cup. Omit cinnamon, nutmeg and salt. Add 1 teaspoon grated orange zest with the flour, if desired. Substitute 3 cups ½-inch pieces rhubarb and 3 cups sliced fresh strawberries for the apples. Decrease butter to 1 tablespoon. Bake pie 50 to 55 minutes or just until juices begin to bubble through crust.

TWO-CRUST PASTRY

8 SERVINGS   PREP TIME: **20 MINUTES**   START TO FINISH: **1 HOUR 5 MINUTES**

2   **cups plus 2 tablespoons all-purpose flour**

1   **teaspoon salt**

²/₃ **cup cold shortening**

6   **to 8 tablespoons ice-cold water**

1. In medium bowl, mix flour and salt. Cut in shortening, using pastry blender or fork, until mixture forms coarse crumbs the size of small peas. Sprinkle with water, 1 tablespoon at a time, tossing with fork until all flour is moistened and pastry almost leaves side of bowl (1 to 2 teaspoons more water can be added if necessary).

2. Gather pastry into a ball. Divide pastry in half and shape into 2 rounds on lightly floured surface. Wrap flattened rounds in plastic wrap and refrigerate 45 minutes or until dough is firm and cold, yet pliable. (This allows the shortening to become slightly firm, which helps make the baked pastry flaky. If refrigerated longer, let pastry soften slightly at room temperature before rolling.)

3. Using floured rolling pin, roll 1 pastry round on lightly floured surface (or pastry board with floured pastry cloth) into round 2 inches larger than upside-down 9-inch glass pie plate. Fold pastry into fourths and place in pie plate, or roll pastry loosely around rolling pin and transfer to pie plate. Unfold or unroll pastry and ease into plate, pressing firmly against bottom and side and being careful not to stretch pastry, which will cause it to shrink when baked.

4. Spoon desired filling into bottom crust. Trim overhanging edge of bottom crust ½ inch from rim of plate.

5. Roll out second pastry round. Fold into fourths and place over filling, or roll loosely around rolling pin and place over filling. Unfold or unroll pastry over filling. Cut slits in top pastry so steam can escape.

6. Trim overhanging edge of top pastry 1 inch from rim of plate. Fold edge of top crust under bottom crust, forming a stand-up rim of pastry that is even thickness on edge of pie plate, pressing on rim to seal; flute edges (see Pastry Edge Treatments, page 258). Bake as directed in pie recipe.

1 SERVING: CALORIES 290; TOTAL FAT 20G (SATURATED FAT 5G, TRANS FAT 0G); CHOLESTEROL 0MG; SODIUM 300MG; TOTAL CARBOHYDRATE 25G (DIETARY FIBER 1G); PROTEIN 3G **EXCHANGES:** 1 STARCH, ½ OTHER CARBOHYDRATE, 4 FAT **CARBOHYDRATE CHOICES:** 1½

TIPS FOR MAKING TENDER, FLAKY PIE PASTRY

- See Measuring Ingredients (page 195).
- Cut the shortening into the flour using a pastry blender or potato masher until the mixture forms coarse, pea-sized crumbs.
- Alternatively, use a fork to cut in the shortening; however, a fork will take longer to make the pea-sized crumbs.
- Use cold water—sprinkling 1 tablespoon at a time over the pastry ingredients and tossing with the flour mixture before adding another tablespoon.
- Add just enough water until pastry almost leaves the side of the bowl.
- Shaping pastry into rounds helps make it a lot easier to roll the dough. When forming the rounds, try to lightly press back together any cracks that form.
- In order to get a tender, flaky crust, work with the dough as little as possible.
- To transfer pastry to a pie plate, gently fold the dough into fourths. Line up the point of the dough with the center of the pie plate; gently unfold dough.

TECHNIQUES AND VARIATIONS ▶

TWO-CRUST PASTRY (CONTINUED)

PASTRY EDGE TREATMENTS

It's important that the bottom and top crusts are well sealed to prevent the filling from escaping through gaps while baking. Seal the edge as directed in Two-Crust Pastry (page 256). Then make the edge attractive by using one of these treatments:

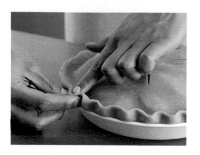

SCALLOPED EDGE

Place thumb and index finger about 1 inch apart on outside of raised edge. With other index finger, push pastry toward outside, continuing around edge, repeating motion, to form scalloped edge.

ROPE OR PINCHED EDGE

Place side of thumb on pastry rim at angle. Pinch pastry by pressing knuckle of index finger down into pastry toward thumb. Continue around edge, repeating motion, to form rope edge.

FORK OR HERRINGBONE EDGE

Dip fork tines in flour; press fork diagonally onto edge without pressing through pastry. Continue motion around edge of pastry for fork pattern. For herringbone pattern, after pressing the tines down once, rotate tines 90 degrees and press again next to the first set of marks. Continue motion around edge of pastry, rotating tines back and forth.

Variations

BUTTER CRUST
Prepare as directed—except substitute cold butter, cut into ½-inch pieces, for half of the shortening.

GLAZED CRUST
Brush top pastry lightly with beaten egg or egg yolk mixed with 1 teaspoon water before baking.

SHINY TOP CRUST
Brush top pastry lightly with milk before baking.

SUGARY CRUST
Brush top pastry lightly with water or milk, and sprinkle with granulated sugar or white coarse sugar crystals before baking.

GLAZE FOR BAKED PIE
In small bowl, mix ½ cup powdered sugar, 2 to 3 teaspoons milk, orange juice or lemon juice and, if desired, 2 teaspoons grated orange or lemon peel. Brush or drizzle over warm baked pie crust, but do not let glaze run over edge of pie.

LEMON CHEESECAKE
with Fresh Berry Topping

16 SERVINGS   PREP TIME: **30 MINUTES**   START TO FINISH: **9 HOURS**

CRUST

- 1¾ **cups crushed gingersnap cookies (about 35 cookies)**
- 6 **tablespoons butter, melted**
- 1 **tablespoon brown sugar**

FILLING

- 3 **packages (8 oz each) cream cheese, softened**
- ¾ **cup granulated sugar**
- 3 **eggs**
- ½ **cup whipping cream**
- 2 **tablespoons grated lemon zest**
- 3 **tablespoons fresh lemon juice**

TOPPING AND GARNISH

- 1 **cup Sweetened Whipped Cream (page 242)**
- ½ **cup fresh blueberries**
- ½ **cup fresh raspberries**
- **Lemon twists**

1. Heat oven to 350°F. Wrap outside bottom and side of 9-inch springform pan with heavy-duty foil. Spray inside bottom and side of pan with cooking spray. In medium bowl, mix crust ingredients. Press mixture in bottom of pan. Bake 5 to 7 minutes or until set. Cool 5 minutes. Reduce oven temperature to 300°F.

2. In large bowl, beat cream cheese and granulated sugar with electric mixer on medium speed 2 minutes. Beat in eggs, one at a time, just until blended. On low speed, beat in whipping cream and lemon zest and juice. Pour over crust. Bake for 1 hour to 1 hour 10 minutes or until edge of cheesecake is set at least 2 inches from edge of pan but center still jiggles slightly. Run small metal spatula around edge of pan. Turn oven off; open oven door 4 inches. Leave cheesecake in oven 30 minutes. Cool in pan on cooling rack 30 minutes. Cover and refrigerate 6 hours or overnight.

3. Just before serving, run small metal spatula around edge of pan; remove side of pan. Spoon whipped cream onto cheesecake. Top with berries and lemon twists. Store covered in refrigerator.

1 SERVING: CALORIES 350; TOTAL FAT 26G (SATURATED FAT 14G, TRANS FAT 1G); CHOLESTEROL 110MG; SODIUM 280MG; TOTAL CARBOHYDRATE 25G (DIETARY FIBER 0G); PROTEIN 5G **EXCHANGES:** ½ STARCH, 1 OTHER CARBOHYDRATE, ½ HIGH-FAT MEAT, 4 ½ FAT **CARBOHYDRATE CHOICES:** 1½

Techniques

WHAT IS A SPRINGFORM PAN?

A springform pan is a deep, round pan with a removable outer ring that is used for foods that can't be turned upside down to be removed from a pan, such as cheesecake.

HOW TO MAKE A BEAUTIFUL CHEESECAKE

- Pressing the crust over the bottom of the springform pan is easiest if you take the side of the pan off first. Reassemble the pan after pressing in the bottom crust.
- Wrapping the bottom and outside of the pan with foil will help keep any cheesecake mixture that leaks from the pan from burning on the bottom of your oven.
- Heavy-duty foil from a wide roll is the best type of foil to use when wrapping the pan.
- Doneness can be tricky with cheesecakes. If underbaked, the cheesecake won't hold its shape when cut. If it's overbaked, large cracks can form on top of the cheesecake.
- Start with the minimum bake time and check for doneness by using the indicators stated in the recipe. Bake longer if necessary, a few minutes at a time, until the doneness is achieved.
- Cooling cheesecake can also cause cracks. Be sure to follow the cooling directions in the recipe exactly to avoid cracks.
- Without releasing the side of the pan, run a small metal spatula around the side of the pan to loosen the baked cheesecake.

VARIATIONS ▶

Variations

ALMOND CHEESECAKE WITH FRESH BERRY TOPPING
Prepare as directed—except substitute 1 teaspoon almond extract for the lemon zest and lemon juice. Add ¼ cup sliced almonds with the berries.

COCONUT-LEMON CHEESECAKE
Prepare as directed—except substitute ½ cup flake coconut for the berries.

DOUBLE VANILLA CHEESECAKE
Prepare as directed—except in the crust, substitute crushed vanilla wafer cookies (about 52) for the gingersnaps and omit sugar. In the filling, substitute 2 teaspoons vanilla for the lemon zest and juice. In the topping and garnish, substitute 4 chopped toffee candy bars (about 1.4 ounces each) for the berries and lemon twists.

LEMON CHEESECAKE WITH CHERRY TOPPING
Prepare as directed—except substitute 1 cup cherry pie filling (from 21-ounce can) for the fresh berries.

ORANGE CHEESECAKE WITH BERRY TOPPING
Prepare as directed—except substitute orange zest and fresh orange juice for the lemon zest and lemon juice.

LEMON SCHAUM TORTE

8 SERVINGS   PREP TIME: **35 MINUTES**   START TO FINISH: **17 HOURS 5 MINUTES**

MERINGUE SHELL

3	**egg whites**
¼	**teaspoon cream of tartar**
¾	**cup sugar**

FILLING

¾	**cup sugar**
3	**tablespoons cornstarch**
¼	**teaspoon salt**
¾	**cup water**
3	**egg yolks, slightly beaten**
1	**tablespoon butter**
1	**teaspoon grated lemon zest**
⅓	**cup fresh lemon juice**

TOPPING AND GARNISH

1	**cup heavy whipping cream**
1	**package (6 oz) fresh raspberries**

1. Heat oven to 275°F. Line cookie sheet with cooking parchment paper. In medium bowl, beat egg whites and cream of tartar with electric mixer on high speed until foamy. Beat in ¾ cup sugar, 1 tablespoon at a time; continue beating until stiff peaks form and mixture is glossy. Do not underbeat. On cookie sheet, shape meringue into 9-inch round with back of spoon, building up side.

2. Bake 1 hour 30 minutes. Turn off oven; leave meringue in oven with door closed 1 hour. Finish cooling at room temperature, about 2 hours.

3. In 2-quart saucepan, mix ¾ cup sugar, the cornstarch and salt. Gradually stir in water. Cook over medium heat, stirring constantly, until mixture thickens and boils. Boil and stir 1 minute. Gradually stir at least half of the hot mixture into egg yolks; stir back into hot mixture in saucepan. Boil and stir 1 minute; remove from heat.

4. Stir in butter, lemon zest and lemon juice. Press plastic wrap onto surface to keep it from drying out. Cool to room temperature. Spoon into meringue shell. Cover and refrigerate at least 12 hours but no longer than 24 hours.

5. In chilled medium bowl, beat whipping cream with electric mixer on high speed until soft peaks form. Spread over filling. Refrigerate until serving. Garnish with raspberries. Store in refrigerator.

1 SERVING: CALORIES 300; TOTAL FAT 13G (SATURATED FAT 7G, TRANS FAT 0G); CHOLESTEROL 105MG; SODIUM 120MG; TOTAL CARBOHYDRATE 45G (DIETARY FIBER 1G); PROTEIN 3G **EXCHANGES:** 1 STARCH, 2 OTHER CARBOHYDRATE, 2½ FAT **CARBOHYDRATE CHOICES:** 3

MERINGUE SHELL TIPS

- See Separating Eggs, page 269.
- Bake the meringue shell until it's completely dry to prevent it from becoming soft.
- Cool the meringue in the turned-off oven for as long as the recipe directs so it is dry and crisp.
- Store the meringue tightly covered.
- Fill the meringue just before serving to keep it crisp.

WHY DOES MERINGUE WEEP?

If not properly made and handled, meringues can weep. Weeping is when droplets of moisture bead up on the surface of the meringue, making it sticky and soft. Use these tricks to keep meringue from weeping:

- Make meringues on non-humid days.
- Beat in the sugar a little at a time to ensure that it's completely dissolved.
- Don't overbake meringue or the egg whites can shrink, squeezing water out so that the meringue weeps.
- Cool the meringue completely before filling.

MAKING CUSTARD AND WHIPPED CREAM

See Making a Custard (page 277).
See Making Whipped Cream (page 273).

VARIATIONS ▶

Variations

BANANA-CHOCOLATE MERINGUE TORTE

Prepare as directed—except omit Filling. Line bottom of cooled meringue shell with sliced banana. Fill cooled meringue shell with prepared chocolate pudding. Continue as directed in step 5.

CHERRY-BERRIES MERINGUE TORTE

Prepare as directed—except omit Filling. Substitute 1 cup sliced strawberries for the raspberries. In large bowl, mix 3 ounces softened cream cheese and ½ cup sugar. Prepare whipped cream as directed in step 5—except fold in 1 cup miniature marshmallows. Fold marshmallow mixture into cream cheese mixture. Spread whipped cream mixture in cooled meringue shell. Toss strawberries with 1 can (21 ounces) cherry pie filling and 1 teaspoon fresh lemon juice; spoon over whipped cream mixture.

CREAMY PEACH MERINGUE TORTE

Prepare as directed—except omit Filling. Substitute 2 sliced peeled peaches for the raspberries. In medium bowl, mix 3 containers (6 ounces each) peach yogurt with 1 package (4-serving size) instant vanilla pudding and pie filling on low speed until blended. Spread in cooled meringue shell. Top with whipped cream. Cover and refrigerate at least 8 hours but no longer than 24 hours. Garnish with peaches.

LEMON-RASPBERRY MERINGUE TORTE

Prepare as directed—except while meringue shell is cooling, in 2-quart saucepan, mix ¼ cup sugar and 2 tablespoons cornstarch. Drain and reserve juice from 1 bag (12 ounces) thawed frozen raspberries. If necessary, add water to measure ½ cup; gradually add raspberry liquid to sugar mixture. Cook and stir over medium heat until thickened. Gently fold in raspberries. Cool; spoon into cooled meringue shell. Continue as directed in step 3.

TRUFFLE-FILLED PEPPERMINT MERINGUE TORTE

Prepare as directed—except add ¼ teaspoon each peppermint extract and red food color with the sugar in meringue shell. Omit Filling. Substitute ¼ cup crushed peppermint candies for the raspberries. In 2-quart heavy saucepan, heat ½ cup heavy whipping cream over medium-low heat just to simmering. Remove from heat; stir in 1 cup dark chocolate chips with wire whisk until melted. Stir in ¼ cup butter cut into small pieces, a few at a time, until melted. Refrigerate until thickened, about 30 minutes. Fill cooled meringue shell with truffle mixture. Continue as directed in step 5.

60

CHOCOLATE MOUSSE

8 SERVINGS   PREP TIME: **20 MINUTES**   START TO FINISH: **2 HOURS 20 MINUTES**

4 **egg yolks**

¼ **cup sugar**

2½ **cups heavy whipping cream**

8 **oz semisweet or dark baking chocolate, chopped**

1. In small bowl, beat egg yolks with electric mixer on high speed 3 minutes or until thick and lemon colored. Gradually beat in sugar.

2. In 2-quart saucepan, heat 1 cup whipping cream over medium heat just until hot. Gradually stir at least half of the hot cream into egg yolk mixture, then stir back into hot cream in saucepan. Cook over low heat about 5 minutes, stirring constantly, until mixture thickens (do not boil).

3. Stir in chocolate until melted. Cover and refrigerate about 2 hours, stirring occasionally, just until chilled.

4. In chilled large, deep bowl, beat remaining 1½ cups whipping cream with electric mixer on low speed until mixture begins to thicken. Gradually increase speed to high and beat until stiff peaks form. Fold chocolate mixture into whipped cream.

5. Pipe or spoon mixture into 8 dessert dishes or stemmed glasses. Refrigerate until serving. Store covered in refrigerator.

1 SERVING: CALORIES 460; TOTAL FAT 41G (SATURATED FAT 24G, TRANS FAT 0.5G); CHOLESTEROL 190MG; SODIUM 35MG; TOTAL CARBOHYDRATE 17G (DIETARY FIBER 4G); PROTEIN 6G **EXCHANGES:** ½ STARCH, ½ OTHER CARBOHYDRATE, ½ MEDIUM-FAT MEAT, 7½ FAT **CARBOHYDRATE CHOICES:** 1

Techniques

SEPARATING EGGS

Crack each egg, one at a time, over a custard cup or small bowl before adding to the bowl that you'll use to beat the eggs. This way, if any pieces of shell get into the eggs, it's easier to remove them from one egg than it is to fish them out of a bowlful.

1. Crack the center of the egg on the edge of the counter by hitting the counter with one good blow. Try not to hit the egg so hard that it shatters the shell in small pieces but rather make one good crack in the center of the shell.
2. Over a custard cup, open the egg and separate the shell into two halves with your thumbs. Leave the egg in a shell; don't let the egg slip into the custard cup at this point.
3. Transfer the egg between the halves, allowing the white to fall into the custard cup while the yolk remains in a shell. Use the sharp edge of the shells to help separate the white from the yolk.
4. When only the yolk is left in a shell, pour the yolk into the bowl you'll use for beating all the yolks.
5. Discard the shell. Check the custard cup for any shell pieces; remove and discard. Transfer the egg white to a storage container.

Whites can be covered and refrigerated for scrambled egg whites or to bulk up scrambled whole eggs. Use within a day or two.

TEMPERING EGGS

Tempering is done to egg yolk mixtures to prevent them from getting clumpy. Hot liquid is stirred into the egg yolks before cooking the mixture.

HOW TO TEMPER EGGS

1. Beat eggs as directed in recipe.
2. Heat liquid until hot.
3. Gradually add at least half of the hot liquid to the egg yolks, stirring constantly.
4. Stir egg yolk mixture back into remaining hot liquid, stirring constantly.

See Making Whipped Cream (page 273).

VARIATIONS ▶

Variations

CHOCOLATE MOUSSE PIE
Prepare as directed through step 4—except double the ingredients and use a 4-quart saucepan. Spoon mousse into a prepared chocolate cookie crust. Prepare Sweetened Whipped Cream (page 242); spread over mousse. Cover lightly and refrigerate 3 to 4 hours or until set.

CHOCOLATE-ALMOND MOUSSE
Prepare as directed—except add ¼ teaspoon almond extract with the whipping cream. Serve chilled mousse topped with whipped cream and toasted slivered almonds.

DOUBLE CHOCOLATE MOUSSE
Prepare as directed—except top mousse with white chocolate curls or shavings before refrigerating in step 5.

MOCHA MOUSSE
Prepare as directed—except add 2 teaspoons instant coffee granules or crystals with the whipping cream.

ZEBRA MOUSSE DESSERT
Prepare as directed through step 4. Prepare Sweetened Whipped Cream (page 242) as directed. Layer crushed chocolate wafer cookies, mousse and Sweetened Whipped Cream in stemmed glasses. Cover and refrigerate until serving.

#61

Cold Brew COFFEE PIE

8 SERVINGS   PREP TIME: **55 MINUTES**   START TO FINISH: **16 HOURS 55 MINUTES**

COLD BREW COFFEE MILK

1⅓	cups coarse ground regular or decaffeinated coffee (4 oz)
4	cups milk

CUSTARD

4	egg yolks
⅔	cup sugar
¼	cup cornstarch
¼	teaspoon salt
1½	teaspoons vanilla

COOKIE CRUST

2	cups finely crushed creme-filled chocolate sandwich cookies (about 20 cookies)
3	tablespoons butter, melted

WHIPPED CREAM LAYER

2	cups heavy whipping cream
2	tablespoons sugar
1½	teaspoons vanilla
	Additional finely crushed creme-filled chocolate sandwich cookies crumbs, if desired

1. In medium bowl or large jar, place coffee. Add milk and gently stir; cover. Let stand in refrigerator at least 12 hours but no longer than 18 hours. Pour coffee and grounds through fine-mesh strainer into pitcher (do not stir). Discard solids.

2. In medium bowl, beat egg yolks with fork. In 2-quart saucepan, mix ⅔ cup sugar, the cornstarch and salt, Gradually stir in cold brew coffee milk. Cook over medium heat, stirring constantly, until mixture thickens and boils. Boil and stir 1 minute. Immediately stir about half of the hot mixture gradually into egg yolks; then stir back into hot mixture in pan. Boil and stir 1 minute; remove from heat. Stir in 1½ teaspoons vanilla; cool 15 minutes.

3. Reserve ½ cup crushed cookies; set aside. In medium bowl, mix remaining cookies and the melted butter. Press mixture in bottom and up side of 9-inch glass pie plate. Pour custard mixture into crust. Refrigerate at least 2 hours.

4. Spoon reserved ½ cup crushed cookies over custard. In chilled medium, deep bowl, beat whipping cream, 2 tablespoons sugar and 1½ teaspoons vanilla with electric mixer on low speed until mixture begins to thicken. Gradually increase speed to high until soft peaks form. Spread whipped cream over cookie crumbs. Chill at least 3 hours. Garnish with additional cookie crumbs. Cover and refrigerate any leftover pie no longer than 24 hours.

1 SERVING: CALORIES 540; TOTAL FAT 33G (SATURATED FAT 18G, TRANS FAT 1G); CHOLESTEROL 180MG; SODIUM 300MG; TOTAL CARBOHYDRATE 51G (DIETARY FIBER 1G); PROTEIN 8G **EXCHANGES:** 1½ STARCH, 1½ OTHER CARBOHYDRATE, ½ LOW-FAT MILK, 6 FAT **CARBOHYDRATE CHOICES:** 3½

MAKING COLD BREW COFFEE MILK

- You can make just the Cold Brew Coffee Milk portion of this recipe for a delicious, cold caffeinated beverage, if you like.
- This is the same method used to make cold brewed coffee for drinking. If you wish to make coffee, substitute water for the milk.
- Using a small strainer to strain the coffee grounds from the milk may leave some coffee sediment in the milk, which will add a bit of crunch to the finished pie. If you want a smoother-textured pie, line the strainer with several layers of cheesecloth over a bowl or pitcher to strain more of the coffee grounds from the milk.

MAKING A CUSTARD

See page 277.

MAKING WHIPPED CREAM

- Only heavy whipping cream can be beaten enough to make soft peaks. Light cream and half-and-half don't have enough fat to beat into soft peaks.
- Use a chilled bowl and beaters for the best whipped cream volume. Place them in the freezer or refrigerator 10 to 20 minutes before using.
- Start beating the cream with the electric mixer on low speed to avoid the cream spattering out of the bowl. As it gets thicker, you can gradually increase the speed to high.
- Watch carefully, and stir up the cream from the bottom of the bowl occasionally so that all the cream whips but doesn't over-whip and become curdled.
- To test if the whipped cream has soft peaks, turn off the mixer and lift the beaters out of the cream. If the cream has peaks that fold over but hold their shape, it has been beaten long enough.

VARIATIONS ▶

Variations

BANANA-COLD BREW COFFEE PIE

Prepare as directed—except place a layer of thinly sliced bananas over the cookie crust before adding the custard and another layer over the cookie crumbs before adding the whipped cream. Top pie with additional banana slices just before serving.

CINNAMON-COLD BREW COFFEE PIE

Prepare as directed—except use coarsely ground cinnamon-flavored coffee. Sprinkle each serving with cinnamon-sugar just before serving.

COLD BREW COFFEE PARFAITS

Prepare as directed—except use 8 parfait glasses. Omit butter. Cool coffee mixture as directed; refrigerate in medium bowl 1 to 2 hours or until cool. Layer coffee base, whipped cream, and cookie crumbs in glasses; repeat layers. Chill at least 2 hours or until set.

COLD BREW COFFEE S'MORE SQUARES

Prepare as directed—except omit sandwich cookie crumbs and butter. Arrange 9 graham cracker squares in bottom of 9-inch square dish or pan; place another layer of crackers on top. Spoon coffee mixture on top; chill 2 hours. Spread ¼ cup chocolate syrup over coffee custard. Arrange two more layers of graham crackers on top. Decrease heavy whipping cream to 1 cup and omit sugar and vanilla. Whip cream until soft peaks form; beat in 1 cup marshmallow crème until soft peaks form. Spread over graham crackers. Chill 3 hours. Drizzle with chocolate syrup.

TOASTED COCONUT-COLD BREW COFFEE PIE

Prepare as directed—except fold ⅓ cup toasted flake coconut into the whipped cream before spreading on pie. Sprinkle top of pie with additional toasted coconut with the cookie crumbs.

VANILLA ICE CREAM

1 QUART   PREP TIME: **10 MINUTES**   START TO FINISH: **2 HOURS 50 MINUTES**

½ **cup sugar**

¼ **teaspoon salt**

1 **cup milk**

3 **egg yolks, slightly beaten**

2 **cups heavy whipping cream**

1 **tablespoon vanilla**

1. In 2-quart saucepan, mix sugar and salt; gradually stir in milk. Cook over medium heat just until mixture comes to a boil. Gradually stir half of the hot milk mixture into egg yolks, stirring constantly. Stir back into remaining milk mixture in pan. Boil and stir 1 minute.

2. Pour milk mixture into chilled bowl. Refrigerate uncovered 2 to 3 hours, stirring occasionally, until room temperature. (At this point, mixture can be refrigerated up to 24 hours before completing recipe if desired.)

3. Stir whipping cream and vanilla into milk mixture. Pour into 1-quart ice-cream freezer; freeze according to manufacturer's directions. Transfer ice cream to storage container. Freeze up to 3 months.

1 SERVING (½ CUP): CALORIES 270; TOTAL FAT 21G (SATURATED FAT 12G, TRANS FAT 0.5G); CHOLESTEROL 150MG; SODIUM 110MG; TOTAL CARBOHYDRATE 16G (DIETARY FIBER 0G); PROTEIN 3G **EXCHANGES:** 1 STARCH, 4 FAT **CARBOHYDRATE CHOICES:** 1

Techniques

TIPS FOR MAKING SMOOTH AND CREAMY ICE CREAM
For a rich, perfect-textured ice cream, start with a chilled custard.

MAKING A CUSTARD
- The protein in eggs is used to thicken milk or cream and sugar. By heating the mixture, it will thicken.
- See Tempering Eggs (page 269).

CHILLING THE MILK MIXTURE
- Be sure to chill the milk mixture at least to room temperature before adding the whipping cream. If possible, make the milk mixture the day before so that it's cold when adding the cold cream. The ice-cream freezer won't have to work as hard, and you'll get ice cream with a nice consistency.
- The ice cream will be soft when it comes out of the ice-cream freezer. You can eat it like it is or let it stand in the ice-cream freezer up to 30 minutes for it to continue to ripen or harden.
- If you like, place scoops of ice cream on a cookie sheet. Freeze until firm, about 20 minutes. Wrap the scoops individually. Freeze up to 3 months.

VARIATIONS ▶

Variations

CHOCOLATE ICE CREAM
Prepare as directed—except increase sugar to 1 cup. Beat 2 ounces unsweetened baking chocolate, melted and cooled, into milk mixture before cooking. Decrease vanilla to 1 teaspoon.

EGGNOG ICE CREAM
Prepare as directed—except add ¼ teaspoon ground nutmeg with the sugar. Add 1 teaspoon rum extract with the vanilla.

FRESH BLUEBERRY ICE CREAM
Prepare as directed—except decrease vanilla to 1 teaspoon. Mash 2 cups fresh blueberries and an additional ⅓ cup sugar with potato masher, or process in food processor, until slightly chunky (not pureed). Stir into milk mixture after adding vanilla.

FRESH PEACH ICE CREAM
Prepare as directed—except decrease vanilla to 1 teaspoon. Mash 4 or 5 fresh peeled peaches with potato masher or process in food processor until slightly chunky (not pureed) to make 2 cups. Stir into milk mixture after adding vanilla.

FRESH RASPBERRY ICE CREAM
Prepare as directed—except substitute ½ teaspoon almond extract for the vanilla. Mash 2 cups fresh raspberries with potato masher or process in food processor until slightly chunky (not pureed); stir into milk mixture after adding almond extract.

Metric Conversion Guide

VOLUME

U.S. UNITS	CANADIAN METRIC	AUSTRALIAN METRIC
¼ teaspoon	1 mL	1 ml
½ teaspoon	2 mL	2 ml
1 teaspoon	5 mL	5 ml
1 tablespoon	15 mL	20 ml
¼ cup	50 mL	60 ml
⅓ cup	75 mL	80 ml
½ cup	125 mL	125 ml
⅔ cup	150 mL	170 ml
¾ cup	175 mL	190 ml
1 cup	250 mL	250 ml
1 quart	1 liter	1 liter
1½ quarts	1.5 liters	1.5 liters
2 quarts	2 liters	2 liters
2½ quarts	2.5 liters	2.5 liters
3 quarts	3 liters	3 liters
4 quarts	4 liters	4 liters

WEIGHT

U.S. UNITS	CANADIAN METRIC	AUSTRALIAN METRIC
1 ounce	30 grams	30 grams
2 ounces	55 grams	60 grams
3 ounces	85 grams	90 grams
4 ounces (¼ pound)	115 grams	125 grams
8 ounces (½ pound)	225 grams	225 grams
16 ounces (1 pound)	455 grams	500 grams
1 pound	455 grams	0.5 kilogram

Note: The recipes in this cookbook have not been developed or tested using metric measures. When converting recipes to metric, some variations in quality may be noted.

MEASUREMENTS

INCHES	CENTIMETERS
1	2.5
2	5.0
3	7.5
4	10.0
5	12.5
6	15.0
7	17.5
8	20.5
9	23.0
10	25.5
11	28.0
12	30.5
13	33.0

TEMPERATURES

FAHRENHEIT	CELSIUS
32°	0°
212°	100°
250°	120°
275°	140°
300°	150°
325°	160°
350°	180°
375°	190°
400°	200°
425°	220°
450°	230°
475°	240°
500°	260°

Index

Page numbers in *italics* indicate illustrations

RECIPE TESTING AND CALCULATING NUTRITION INFORMATION

RECIPE TESTING:

- Large eggs and 2% milk were used unless otherwise indicated.

- Fat-free, low-fat, low-sodium or lite products were not used unless indicated.

- No nonstick cookware and bakeware were used unless otherwise indicated. No dark-colored, black or insulated bakeware was used.

- When a pan is specified, a metal pan was used; a baking dish or pie plate means ovenproof glass was used.

- An electric hand mixer was used for mixing only when mixer speeds are specified.

CALCULATING NUTRITION:

- The first ingredient was used wherever a choice is given, such as 1/3 cup sour cream or plain yogurt.

- The first amount was used wherever a range is given, such as 3- to 3 1/2-pound whole chicken.

- The first serving number was used wherever a range is given, such as 4 to 6 servings.

- "If desired" ingredients were not included.

- Only the amount of a marinade or frying oil that is absorbed was included.

- Diabetic exchanges are not calculated in recipes containing uncooked alcohol, due to its effect on blood sugar levels